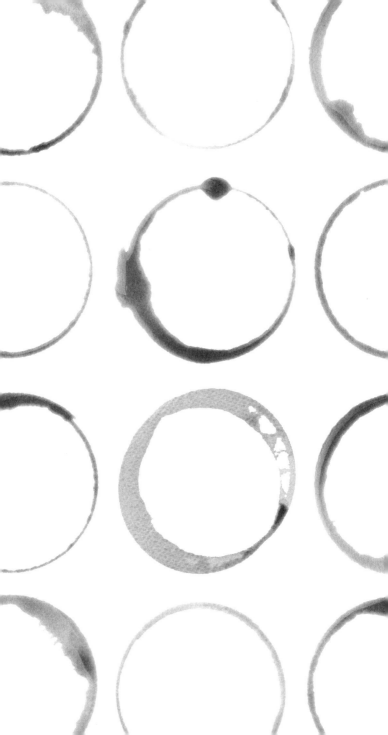

TOP 100 WINES UNDER $20

Had a Glass 2013

JAMES NEVISON

appetite
by RANDOM HOUSE

Appetite by Random House and colophon are
registered trademarks of Random House of Canada Limited

Library and Archives of Canada Cataloguing in Publication is available upon request

ISBN: 978-0-449-01575-9

Food icons by Andrew Roberts. Other images from Shutterstock.com.
Printed and bound in the USA

Published in Canada by Appetite by Random House,
a division of Random House of Canada Limited

www.randomhouse.ca

10 9 8 7 6 5 4 3 2 1

CONTENTS

A Brief Guide to Wine Enjoyment

Had a Glass?

Welcome to Had a Glass. This is the guide for everyday wine enjoyment.

Had a Glass wades through the muck and murky liquid to point out one hundred wines worth sipping. Consider it a vinous compass to keep you from getting lost in the wine aisles. Better yet, all the wines featured on these pages sell for under $20. Because wine is meant for everyday enjoyment, and every meal deserves a glass of wine.

Had a Glass is filled with the straight wine goods. Each wine is here for a reason, whether it is perfect for patio sipping, pairs remarkably with salmon, or simply inspires engagement in impromptu conversation. The wines come from all over the globe and represent a broad mix of grape varieties. There are reds and whites, not to mention rosés and sparkling, even a few fortified wines! It's true wine diversity, and true wine value.

Had a Glass is easy to use: pick a page, read the blurb, get the wine, and see what you think. Repeat.

> **But remember: wine is best enjoyed in moderation. Know your limit and always have a safe way to get home. Such is the path to true wine appreciation.**

Caveat Emptor and Carpe Diem!

Had a Glass goes out of the way to select wines that are widely available. Everyone deserves good wine, no matter what your postal code. While every effort is made to ensure prices and vintages are correct at publication, good wine buys sell out, and wines are subject to price variances and vintage changes.

It is recommended to use this book as a starting point for your wine adventures. Great bottles are out there, and as with all things worth searching for, the fun is in the hunt.

Wine, Barcoded

In a nod to interactivity, this year's edition of Had a Glass features barcodes for each wine. Given the proliferation of smartphones there are all sorts of uses for this handy dandy addition. Using the growing number of available wine "apps," you can scan the barcodes to locate stores and availability for each wine. Or scan your favourite bottles to create your own personalized wine tasting journal!

A Word about Value

"Value" is at best squishy and hard to pin down. Value is personal. And like scoring wine on a hundred-point scale, it's tough for an objective framework to try and prop up subjective tastes. But whether you're after price rollbacks at a big-box store or hand-made designer goods, true value occurs when returns exceed expectations.

How is value applied in Had a Glass?

Most of the time the budget and bank account set the upper limit of my wine allotment at $20. On occasion I may spend more, but overall I toe the line. From research I know the majority of you feel the same. We all love great $18 bottles of wine. But we love cracking into a tasty $12 bottle even more!

Had a Glass celebrates wines that give you the best bottle for your buck: the $10 wine that seems like it should cost $15, the $15 bottle that stands out, and the $20 wine that knocks your socks off. Wine should be an everyday beverage, not a luxury—an enjoyable accessory to good living.

How to Taste Wine

Drinking wine and tasting wine are two different pastimes. Now, there's nothing wrong with simply wanting to open a bottle, pour a glass, and carry on. Indeed most of the time this is standard protocol. Company has arrived and dinner is on the table and away we go!

But if you're ready to take your relationship with wine to the next level, it's time to commit to proper tasting technique. This permits a complete sensory evaluation of the wine in your glass, and I promise that it will add to your wine enjoyment as well.

You've likely heard the motto that a good wine is "a wine you like." Sure, at the end of the day taste is subjective and opinion matters. But what really makes a wine good? After you understand how to taste wine, you'll be equipped to make that call.

The Four Steps

There's no need to overcomplicate wine tasting. Nothing is more boring than listening to some wine blowhard drone on at length about the laundry list of aromas they detect, or slurp on for minutes as they attempt to pinpoint precise acidity and residual sugar levels. First impressions are often the best. Tasting wine is not a competition. It should be fun, which means yes, smile as you swirl and sip.

Here's the wine-tasting process in four simple steps:

Step 1: The look

You can learn a lot simply by looking at a wine. Tilt the wineglass away from you and observe its colour, ideally against a white background (a blank sheet of paper works in a pinch). White wines appear pallid straw to deep gold, and reds typically range from light ruby to the dark crimson of a royal's ceremonial robe—even at times the neon purple of grape Gatorade. A wine's colour can also hint at its age. Young white wines often have the brilliant sheen of white gold, a shine that mellows as the years pass and the wine darkens overall. On the other hand, red wines lighten as they age, superimposing amber and auburn tones on sombre claret. Also consider that while most wines are nearly transparent in the glass, an unfiltered wine may appear slightly cloudy with sediment.

Step 2: The swirl

To draw out a wine's aromas give the glass a swirl. Use the base of a table for secure swirling, or raise your wineglass up high for an air swirl. Before you know it, you'll be swirling every glass in front of you, even if it holds water. The swirl not only helps release the aromas of a wine, it paints the sides of the glass with the wine's tears, or legs. These are the droplets that form around the wineglass and leisurely—or rapidly—make their way to the reservoir waiting at the bottom of the vessel. But note that while a wine's legs are fun to look at, they merely indicate texture and viscosity from residual sugars or alcohol, and don't necessarily suggest a wine's quality.

Step 3: The smell

Don't be afraid to put your nose right into the glass—wine tasting is not chemistry class and we need not adhere to a waft test. Smelling is wine intimacy, and a deep inhale will reveal what the wine is about. Many wine tasters feel the smell is the most important step in "tasting" wine, with scent seemingly hard-wired to our mind.

What are you smelling?

It's not me, it's the Cabernet! Many factors contribute to a wine's aromas, or smells. A wine can have myriad aromas of fruit (citrus, berries, melons, mango), which may at first seem odd considering wine is made from just one fruit: grapes. Wine can smell of place too, be it sun-baked earth, rain-slaked slate, or even horsey barnyard. Of course, the winemaker and winemaking process can also influence a wine's aromas, from the smoke, vanilla, and spice imbued from oak to the yeasty brioche goodness imparted from barrel fermentation and sur lie aging.

It's also important to remember that smell is quite personal. Your apricot may be my peach. And I find the more wines you taste the more comfortable you become addressing aromas. Further, it's not a contest to come up with as many olfactory adjectives as possible—though creativity can be applied in determining what's that smell. (See box on page 8 for examples.)

> But this is the magic of wine,
> the amazing ability of one simple fruit to manifest
> an infinite array of aromas and flavours.

Wine Aromas

Commonly used to describe wine aromas	Unusual-sounding (but actually used) wine aromas
citrus	cat pee
berry	wet stone
peach	burnt match
melon	rubber band
mango	cut grass
bell pepper	barnyard
flowers	baking bread
olive	diesel
nut	Tupperware
caramel	sweat
vanilla	cheese
oak	bacon
smoke	cracked black pepper
earth	tobacco
fig	tar

Step 4: The taste

Finally, take a generous sip of wine (it's fine to slurp as you sip, just as you would a mouthful of steaming ramen noodles!). Swirl it in your mouth. Swish it in your cheeks. Consider the wine's consistency and texture; this is what's referred to as a wine's body. Let your tongue taste the different elements of the wine: any sweetness from residual sugars, any tartness from acid, or any bitterness from alcohol. Tannins may dry your gums, making you pucker. Spitting is optional.

Understanding Body and Finish

Just like hair, wine has body. I find it easiest to think of a wine's body as its texture. And I still find the best analogy for understanding "body" is to think about milk. The consistency may be thin like skim milk (light-bodied) or it may be thick like cream (full-bodied). In the middle of the spectrum we have medium-bodied, the 2% milk of the wine world. Light-, medium-, and full-bodied are the three basic descriptions used, and it's perfectly acceptable to employ a range when describing a wine, say light-to-medium-bodied for example.

However, all good things must come to an end, and a wine's finish refers to the lingering flavours and taste sensations that remain after it's been spit (or swallowed). The jargon is surprisingly simple to describe a wine's finish, which is generally described as short, medium, or long. That said, there's no simple formula for delineating each category. No point in getting out the stopwatch and clocking a wine's finish. In fact, there's no point in getting hung up at all on a wine's finish, better to move on to the next sip.

Wine-Tasting Tips

• Take notes! Whether you carry a leather-bound wine journal or scribble on a paper napkin, take wine notes whenever you can. At the very least, jot down the winery name, grape variety, the year, and a thumbs-up or thumbs-down beside it. (No, you will not remember the wine the next day, other than perhaps that the bottle had a bird on the label.)

• When it comes to glasses, go big. And don't pour it more than half full. This will allow for proper swirling (as per Step 2).

• Practice makes perfect. Like you needed more motivation.

• But it's best not to practise alone. Tasting wine with a companion or group is a great way to gain multiple opinions and perspectives.

Suggested Wine Flights for Wine-Tasting Practice

Wine flights are a great way to practise tasting wine. The more wines you try, the better your frame of reference and the larger your internal wine database. A "flight" of wine lines up small pours of a few wines that share a common theme, allowing for great side-by-side comparison. It's like taking three pairs of jeans into the changing room!

Here are three wine flights for wine-tasting practice:

Flight 1

Yes, Pinot Gris and Pinot Grigio are the same grape. And yes, lately wines made from the grape have become quite fashionable the world over. But no, Pinot Gris(gio) certainly don't all taste the same. Quite the opposite in fact, it's one wine with a dramatic range of styles. This PG flight takes you across the world's wine regions while highlighting the grape's many graces:

Mezzacorona Pinot Grigio, Italy (page 51)
Lurton Pinot Gris, Argentina (page 48)
Wither Hills Pinot Gris, New Zealand (page 75)

Flight 2

Bubbly is one of the most versatile styles of wine around. It's also one of the prettiest, available in every shade imaginable, from barely perceptible light straw through neon purple. But when was the last time you tried a sparkling red? Get effervescent with this flight through the shades of sparkling wine:

White: 1884 Reservado Extra Brut, Argentina (page 143)
Pink: Beato Bartolomeo Breganze "Rosa di Sera" Spumante Extra Dry, Italy (page 144)
Red: Casolari Lambrusco di Sorbara, Italy (page 141)

Flight 3

There are hundreds if not thousands of different grapes used to make wine. But most people can probably count the different types of wine they drink on both hands. Nothing wrong with this, but if you're looking to go beyond the tried and tested, line up this flight of more offbeat reds:

Boutari Naoussa, Greece (page 111)
Niederösterreich Zweigelt, Austria (page 120)
Re Manfredi Aglianico del Vulture, Italy (page 135)

It's the Wine's Fault

Unfortunately, there is likely a point in your wine-tasting journey when you'll encounter a faulty wine. That said, with today's high quality standards, in general there's less bad wine out there. Given our differing thresholds of perception, wine faults may be more or less apparent. But if you open a bottle and think something's funky, it might be due to one of these common wine faults:

- **"Corked" wine or cork taint.** Technically caused by a naturally occurring compound called 2,4,6-trichloroanisole (TCA) found in the oak bark used to produce corks, and attributed to improper cork sanitation. At worst cork taint can leave a wine smelling and tasting mouldy like wet newspaper, but it can also mute flavours and aromas in general.
- **Oxidation.** Too much exposure to oxygen! A wine is particularly susceptible to oxidation after fermentation has completed and carbon dioxide levels have waned. Oxidized wine usually appears brownish in colour and smells stale.
- **Volatile acidity.** When fermentation goes awry, volatile acidity (VA) is usually the end result. VA shows itself in two main ways, through ethyl acetate, which smells like nail polish remover, or acetic acid—good ol' vinegar!
- **Too much SO_2.** The overwhelming majority of wines contain sulphur dioxide, which serves as a preservative and keeps wine stable. Some sulphur dioxide occurs naturally during the winemaking process, but most wineries also add sulphur dioxide. How much is a question of principle and philosophy, but if your wine smells like rotten eggs, it's faulty. If it has just a hint of sulphur dioxide, like a just-lit match, it may blow off and be fine.
- **Brettanomyces.** A funky, naturally occurring yeast behind such colourful wine descriptions as "Band-Aid" and "sweaty horse." Brettanomyces, or Brett, comes from the vineyard and can establish itself in the winery and winery equipment, especially if proper sanitation is not employed. But here's the rub: Brett gets personal. Some wine tasters like a little Brettanomyces in their wine and feel it adds character and complexity—but too much is funky gone off the railroad tracks.

Notes

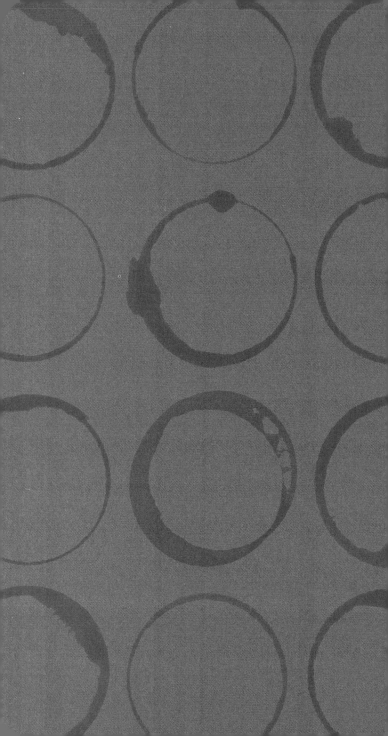

How to Buy Wine

Buying a bottle of wine shouldn't raise heart rates or cause palms to sweat. Wine is fun, and strolling through your local bottle shop should be a joy. Wine-buying confidence has come a long way in the past decade, but there's no harm in offering a few tips to help your troll of the wine aisles.

Navigating the Wine Store

The typical liquor store or wine shop organizes its wine by country. This is helpful categorization if you're feeling geographic, but somewhat awkward if you want a Chardonnay and have to run around comparing one country's offering to another. Things can get particularly unruly if you head to a section with

French or Italian wines and are confronted with regional names emblazoned across the labels instead of the types of grape. No reason to panic (in fact many traditional wine labels are starting to include the grapes along with the region). Get to know where certain grapes come from, and you'll be sleuthing through bottles in no time.

Where does wine come from?

Grapes are grown and wine is made in well over a hundred countries. Entire books are written to cover the various wine regions of the world. This will not be another one. However, a quick primer can provide down-and-dirty generalizations to help you on your way to grape globetrotting.

Old World vs. New World

Before even delving into specific countries, it's important to discuss the Old World and New World of wine. Broadly speaking, the Old World refers to those countries around the Mediterranean basin that have thousands of years of grape-growing and wine-drinking history. We're talking France, Italy, Spain, Portugal, Germany, Austria, Hungary, Greece, et al. The rest of the globe's viticultural hotspots fall into the New World camp.

Traditionally, Old World wines have been typified as more austere and terroir, or place, driven. This is why the wines are usually labelled according to region rather than grape. New World wines tend to get labelled fruit-forward, ripe, and extroverted.

Of course, generalizations are handy but simplistic, and today the line between Old and New World has certainly blurred. You'll find French wines with cute marketing and grape names prominently displayed, and you'll find Chilean bottles touting adherence to Old World–style dry farming and wild yeast fermentation.

The key take-away? It's great to be a wine drinker in this Postmodern World, as the quality (and type) of wine widely available has never been better.

GrapeWHERE

So what happened to the Pinot Gris and Merlot on the label?
Don't fret if you don't see familiar grape names listed on the front of that
bottle from _____ {insert "Old World" country}.
Just remember this is where you'll find different grapes:

WHERE	Grape(s)

White wines

Bordeaux, France	Sémillon and Sauvignon Blanc
Burgundy, France	Chardonnay
Cava, Spain	Macabeo, Parellada, and Xarel-lo
Champagne, France	Chardonnay, Pinot Noir, and Pinot Meunier
Côtes du Rhône, France	Roussanne, Marsanne, and Viognier
Gavi, Italy	Cortese
Mosel, Germany	Riesling
Rioja, Spain	Viura (a.k.a. Macabeo)

Red wines

Barbaresco, Italy	Nebbiolo
Barolo, Italy	Nebbiolo
Beaujolais, France	Gamay
Bordeaux, France	Cabernet Sauvignon, Merlot, and Cabernet Franc (and maybe a little Malbec and Petit Verdot)
Burgundy, France	Pinot Noir
Cahors, France	Malbec
Chianti, Italy	Sangiovese
Côtes du Rhône, France	Mostly Syrah and Grenache, with Carignan, Mourvèdre and Cinsault
Rioja, Spain	Tempranillo, Garnacha
Valpolicella, Italy	Corvina

Understanding Wine Labels

What's written on the wine label counts. You can learn a lot about a wine before you buy. The trick is to know what's worth reading. Wine label literacy can go a long way toward increasing wine enjoyment.

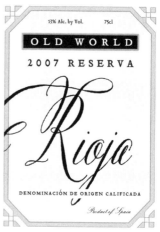

Wine or winery name

Back in the day, the name would be a château or domaine, or possibly it would be a proprietary name that was used by a winemaking co-operative. While these labels are still out there, brand names, animal species, and focus-grouped marketing buzzwords are now gracing wine bottles—all in an effort to help you remember what you drank.

Vintage

The year printed on the label is the year the grapes were grown. There are good years and bad years, typically determined by weather conditions.

The vintage is included for the wines reviewed in Had a Glass. Where no vintage is listed, the wine is "non-vintage," meaning it's been made from a mix of years. Non-vintage is quite common for sparkling and fortified wines.

Alcohol

Generally expressed as "alcohol by volume" (ABV), this tells you how much wine you can taste before the line between "tasting" and "drinking" becomes blurred. Or blurry. As a rough guide, higher alcohol content (14 percent is high, anything above 14.5 percent is really high) suggests a heftier, more intense wine. On the other side of the ABV spectrum, wines with less than 11 percent will often be off-dry (slightly sweet). High alcohol doesn't connote a better wine. It's all about balance, and regardless of the number, a wine shouldn't have the grating bitterness of alcohol—it's not supposed to taste like a vodka shot.

Appellation

Or, where the grapes came from. Old World wine often gives you the appellation instead of the grape variety. But appellations will also inform you about the grapes in the bottle. (See the chart on page 17.) Take an example from Spain. "Rioja," arguably the country's most famous appellation, describes where the grapes originated, and because Spanish appellation laws state only certain grapes are authorized in certain areas, the name also hints at what grapes made the wine. So, appellations (Burgundy, Chianti, Mosel) also help to define taste.

Appellations Around the World

When it comes to appellations, each country has its own terminology. Here are the common formal designations you'll see on wine labels, which indicate that the grapes used to produce the wine originated in the demarcated region.

Country	Regional Designation
France	Appellation d'Origine Contrôlée (AOC or AC)
Italy	Denominazione di Origine Controllata (DOC)
Spain	Denominación de Origen (DO)
Portugal	Denominação de Origem Controlada (DOC)
Chile	Denominación de Origen (DO)
Australia	Geographical Indication (GI)
South Africa	Wine of Origin (WO)
United States	American Viticultural Area (AVA)
Canada	Designated Viticultural Area (DVA), regulated by the Vintners Quality Alliance (VQA)

Grape variety

You pick up a can of soup and it's "mushroom" or "tomato." On a wine bottle you often see the grape variety: Malbec or Merlot or Chardonnay, to mention a few. These are your single varietal wines, as opposed to "blended" wines which combine two or more grapes (such as Cabernet-Merlot and Sémillon–Sauvignon Blanc). Keep in mind that single varietal wines are no better than blends, and vice versa. Preference is dictated by your taste buds.

Occasional Wine

Of course, regardless of how the wines are organized, we often buy a bottle for a certain occasion, be it to pair with Mom's meatloaf or to celebrate Sarah's birthday. This is a logical way to buy wine, especially—ahem—for the occasional wine drinker. But do you match the wine to the food or match the food to the wine? The answer will affect your wine-buying decision.

GrapeWHEN

Grape	WHEN
White wines	
Chardonnay	roast chicken, crab drizzled in butter
Chenin Blanc	pasta alfredo, satay
Gewürztraminer	curry, salad
Pinot Blanc	shrimp cocktail, minestrone
Pinot Gris	smoked salmon, brie
Riesling	rillette, turkey
Sauvignon Blanc	goat cheese, fried chicken
Sémillon	clams, pasta primavera
Torrontés	on its own, Peking duck
Viognier	halibut, ginger beef
Champagne	with strawberries
Red wines	
Cabernet Franc	pork roast, vegetarian lasagna
Cabernet Sauvignon	porterhouse, kebabs
Carmenère	eggplant, grilled beef
Gamay	tacos, turkey
Malbec	venison, mixed grill
Merlot	Camembert, mushrooms
Pinotage	bison, goulash
Pinot Noir	salmon, duck
Sangiovese	lasagna, pizza
Shiraz	lamb, pecorino
Tempranillo	steak, bacon
Zinfandel	burgers, teriyaki
Port	in a cozy chair with a book

Feel the Wine

There's nothing wrong with getting emotional with wine, and another buying strategy is to match the wine to mood. When staring at a wall of wine wondering what to put in the basket, consult your mood ring or do a quick self-emotive audit. Perhaps a bold evening calls for an aggressive wine, just as a mellow affair may require an equally subdued bottle? Looking for a little comfort? Head back to the tried-and-true.

Feeling	Try	From
adventurous	Riesling	Germany, B.C., or Australia
mellow	Pinot Noir	France or California
assertive	Shiraz	Australia or Washington
apathetic	Chardonnay	anywhere
it's complicated	Cabernet blend	Chile or Argentina

Broadening Wine Horizons

While still on the topic of feelings, if you're feeling a bit adventurous, now is the perfect time to experiment with a never-before-tasted wine.

Like	Try	From
Malbec	Pinotage	South Africa
Cabernet Sauvignon	Tempranillo	Spain
Shiraz	Nero d'Avola	Italy
Chardonnay	Viognier	France
Sauvignon Blanc	Grüner Veltliner	Austria
Gewürztraminer	Ehrenfelser	B.C.

The Role of Vintages

Just when you think you're getting to know the nuances of a particular wine, along comes a new vintage! This is in fact one of the more exciting aspects of fermented grape juice. Wine is an agricultural product, subject to the annual vagaries of Mother

Nature. If you want your wine to be the same year in and year out, you may as well buy Welch's. But how important is a wine's vintage?

A general rule is that it's easier to make good wine in a great year, but great grape-growers and winemakers can make good wine every year. A good vintage typically means great to ideal growing conditions: no untimely frosts, plenty of sun to encourage full and even ripening, and so on. That said, in a poor vintage, steps can be taken to minimize negative impacts.

So the vintage of a wine matters, but not to the point that it should limit your wine purchase. Indeed, for everyday wine drinking vintages are usually not really considered. Now if you were investing in wine or looking to purchase bottles at an auction it would be a different story, but those aren't the types of wine you'll find in the pages of Had a Glass.

Corks vs. Screw Caps

There was a time, and we're still talking the 21st century, when a significant proportion of wine drinkers would rather drink water than be seen sipping from a bottle of screw-capped wine. Thankfully it hasn't taken long for most to realize that pulling a cork out of a bottle is only romantic until the first corked bottle, which seems to happen when there is no backup bottle at hand! And with an estimated 5 percent of wines with a cork subject to taint, this is a failure rate no other industry would rightfully tolerate.

So unless you're looking to cellar a wine for a particularly lengthy period of time, or you're risk-seeking and own an impressive collection of corkscrews, embrace the screw cap as an effective, efficient flavour saver. Anyways, it's not like corks are going to completely disappear anytime soon. Just don't be afraid to buy a wine based on its topper!

Bag-in-the-Box, the New Screw Cap!

Now that the screw-cap debate has wound down, the new frontier in packaging is "wine casks," or bag-in-the-box. These nearly indestructible vessels not only make great backcountry travel partners, they're also more environmentally friendly and create an airtight seal to help keep wine fresh longer. Don't be surprised to see more plus-sized casks arriving on wine shelves.

Returning Wine

If a wine is faulty, take it back! Generally this will be due to cork taint, though there is potential for other faults. (See page 12 for a review of common wine faults.) Just don't drink most of the bottle before bringing it back to the store! And no, it is not acceptable to return a wine simply because you do not like the way it tastes. Chalk it up to experience, take notes ruminating on your unmet expectations, and move on to the next bottle.

Avoid a Wine Rut

Becoming a little too comfortable with a certain bottle? It's great to have favourite go-to wines, but remember that it's a wide wine world. If your wining has been monotonous of late, consider these strategies on your next trip to the wine store.

Explore new wine frontiers

When you find yourself infatuated by a particular grape—be it cheerful Chenin Blanc or sumptuous Shiraz—expand on your interest by seeking similar bottles from around the wine world.

Riesling is renowned as a wine capable of showcasing terroir, able to deftly transmit a sense of place directly from the vineyard to the wineglass. Try travelling around the globe in the comfort of home with these three bottles: start in Riesling's historic home of Germany with St. Urbans-Hof (page 72), then head to Washington's Columbia Valley for a taste of Chateau Ste. Michelle (page 60). Finally, end back in B.C. with the homegrown Wild Goose Riesling (page 65).

Get a lay of the land

Certain parts of the world make certain types of wine. Cooler climate areas typically produce wines with higher levels of acidity, and conversely, warmer regions tend to produce riper grapes that manifest in rich, fruit-forward wines. This sense of place imbued in wine is one of the beverage's more enduring traits. Flipping through the pages, you'll see some great wine regions represented this year.

For example, Chile has really embraced wine diversity and vineyards are continually being established (or rehabilitated) in different areas throughout the country. Sip through a few of these exciting subregions by tasting De Martino's Chardonnay (Limarí Valley, page 69) and Caliterra's Tributo Sauvignon Blanc (Leyda Valley, page 68). Then head over to the Puente Alto Vineyard in the Maipo Valley via Concha y Toro's Marques de Casa Concha Cabernet Sauvignon (page 132).

> **The point is, if you like the wine of a particular area or appellation, try others from the same locale.**

Trade up

A winery commonly makes different tiers of wines, akin to a vinous version of Honda versus Acura. *Had a Glass* is all about the everyday sipper, but if you like what you're test driving, look for the luxury version.

Chapoutier has vineyards throughout France, along with a reputation for crafting delicious wines at a variety of price points. Chapoutier's Bila-Haut Blanc (page 56) hails from the Côtes du Roussillon region in southern France and at ~$15 it makes a great everyday white for the dinner table. But if you head to the Rhône you'll find many more wines from Chapoutier, including the tasty Les Granits from Saint Joseph (~$62). Finally, there's always the delectable Chapoutier De l'Orée Ermitage Blanc (~$185) for those special occasions!

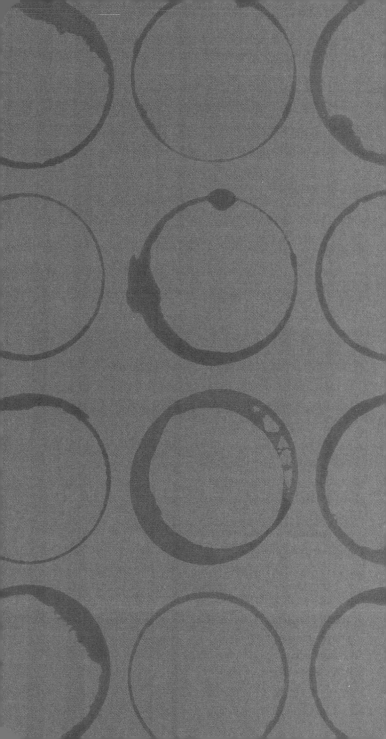

How to Enjoy Wine

Wine is like golf. There is a huge array of specialized accessories. But all you really need to play the game is a set of clubs and some balls. Likewise, all you really need to enjoy wine is a bottle and a glass. From there, it's up to you to decide how much you want to invest and how much shelf space you want to devote to storing wine paraphernalia.

Glasses and Stemware

Crystal? Stemless? Plastic tumbler? Mason jar? The wineglass options are varied, and while not all glasses are created equal, drinking wine from any glass can be equally enjoyable.

It's true that you can buy a different glass tailor-made to

each type of wine. While there is no harm in gathering a glass collection, it's definitely not a necessary pursuit to maximize your wine enjoyment. A set of good white and red glasses (Chardonnay- and Bordeaux-shaped make sense) will suffice, and a standardized ISO tasting glass is helpful to really take wine tasting seriously. But at the end of the day, when a wonderful meal is waiting on the table, a simple juice glass works as well!

Good stemware has its benefits

- Swirling wine in the larger bowl common to fancy glasses does wonders for releasing a wine's aromas. And it's best to pour a few fingers at a time to get a proper swirl going.

- Holding a glass by its stem helps keep white wines chilled, and it also keeps grubby fingerprints off the glass!

- A glass with a thin rim certainly provides an elegant tactile sensation.

Note: The stemless wineglasses that have recently become popular may get marked up with fingerprints, but they fit great in the dishwasher!

Decanters

After glasses, the next most important wine accessory is the decanter. It provides both form and function, and is a secret to getting the most out of your wine.

Decanters have typically been associated with old wines, and it is true that decanting old wines to remove the liquid from the sediment will keep your teeth clean. But how often do you find yourself drinking aged wine?

In these contemporary times the best use of a decanter is as a wine time-machine! Use your decanter to decant young wines, allowing them to breathe. Most wines we buy are consumed young—often too young—and decanting will open these wines up, smoothing their fruit and revealing their true character. There's no magic formula for how long to decant a bottle before drinking, and don't be afraid to give the wine a vigorous shake, but as a general rule most red wines take up to an hour in the decanter. Try "airing" lighter reds for half an hour. White wines don't really need to decant unless you just like the look of it.

Anything can be used as a decanter, from a clean teapot to a juice jug. To get serious about your decanter, look for a glass or crystal container with a wide base and a narrow opening. This facilitates swirling, makes for easier pouring, and looks styling on the table!

Corkscrews

Butterfly

T-Bar

Waiter's Friend

Wars have been fought over broken corks. Well perhaps not, but it certainly is disappointing when a cork is mangled and broken into bits at the hand(s) of a bad corkscrew. (Actually, wine—and the supply thereof—has certainly been a fixture in many wars over the years.)

A corkscrew does not have to be intricate or expensive; a good corkscrew simply needs a well-wound worm (the screw part that winds into the cork) and some decent mechanism for leverage. Avoid corkscrews with worms that resemble a drill bit or wood screw, as these culprits typically do more cork ripping than pulling. Past experience shows these latter worms are most often found on the so-called butterfly corkscrew.

Purists might opt for the good old-fashioned T-bar corkscrew, which certainly hints at nostalgia and can make quite the design statement when the worm is grafted to an old hunk of grapevine à la the rustic French fashion. Just be ready for a firm forearm workout, and be prepared to shove the wine bottle between your legs (or feet) for stability and leverage. Gadgetphiles may be drawn to the fancy, pneumatically assisted and gear-operated corkscrews available, which work just fine but tend to cost the equivalent of a couple good bottles.

For the best all-around corkscrew there's no better than the waiter's friend. Resembling a pocket knife, this simple corkscrew is the go-to option for servers and sommeliers the world over. It tirelessly opens wine bottles, and usually includes a small knife for cutting through bottle foils as well as an integrated crown cap opener. The waiter's friend is cheap (they're pretty easy to find at thrift stores for a couple bucks) and effective (never yet met a cork it couldn't beat), and make you look like you mean wine business when looped around your belt.

Collecting Wine

Starting a wine collection is a fantastic way to expand your wine enjoyment. Sure, a fancy cellar with custom millwork, temperature control, and cobwebs-placed-just-so is a beautiful thing, but the 99 percent of us that don't have the space, the resources, or the patience for such a cellar needn't be deterred from collecting wine.

Start your wine collection simply with a bottle each of red, white, and sparkling wine. Keep the white and bubbly in the fridge and replenish as required. This vinous triumvirate ensures you're prepared for any impromptu occasion. Add to this base collection by picking up bottles while travelling, or perhaps track down a wine you had at a restaurant and really enjoyed. The key is to tie the wines to personal experience, which will add to enjoyment when you finally get around to opening a bottle. If the wine will be consumed in a year or two, simply keep it displayed in your wine rack or in the corner of a closet.

Of course it's important to keep wine storage in perspective. More than 90 percent of wine sold today is made for drinking now (or in a week, three weeks, six months). There is wine for aging and there is wine for drinking, and this book is about the latter. But there's no denying that wine evolves as it gets older, and a wine that is made to cellar can metamorphose into a completely different beverage, replete with aroma and flavour nuances not permitted in young wine. Just make sure to do some research if you plan on buying wine to enjoy in decades to come.

A Starter Cellar
Curious about aging wine? Here is a mixed half-case culled from wines reviewed in this book. Put them in a box, place on its side, and shove away in the basement or seldom-used closet and see how they develop in three to five years.

1) Don Pascual Reserve Tannat, Uruguay (page 117)
2) Amalaya Tinto, Argentina (page 130)
3) Ringbolt Margaret River Cabernet Sauvignon, Australia (page 127)
4) Mission Hill Reserve Chardonnay, British Columbia (page 80)
5) Domaine de Vaugondy Vouvray, France (page 77)
6) St. Urbans-Hof Riesling, Germany (page 72)

Wine-Serving Temperatures

red wine	18°C (65°F)	a bit below room temperature
white (and rosé wine)	10°C (50°F)	20 minutes out of the fridge
sparkling and sweet wine	5°C (40°F)	straight from the fridge

Tips
• The above chart provides general guidelines, but personal preference trumps suggestions.

• Lighter red wines (such as Gamay Noir and Valpolicella) are often enjoyable served a bit cooler, especially when the weather is warm. Conversely, richer white wines (such as Chardonnay) show more complexity served a little warmer than usual.

- Err on the side of serving a wine too cold. The bottle will always warm up as it sits on the table.

- If a wine is sweet, serving it cold will make it seem drier and more refreshing.

- All dessert wine should be served at fridge temperature, unless it's red—like port—in which case you should serve it at the same temperature as red wine.

The Dregs, or Leftover Wine

It's true that wine starts to deteriorate once the bottle is opened and the wine is exposed to oxygen. But how much time do you have before the bottle goes bad? Generally, polishing off a bottle the following day—or if you must, even the day after—is fine.

Yes, there are strategies to postponing a wine's demise. All manner of vacuum pumps and inert-gas sprays are available to attempt at keeping O_2 at bay. If you're wary of accumulating any more wine gadgets, you can simply replace the cork or cap and place the bottle in the fridge—whether white, pink, or red—to slow down the oxidation.

If all this sounds like a lot of effort, you may simply be better off breaking out a chunk of cheese and pouring the dregs around!

Notes

Food and Wine

Wine without food is like treble without bass. Sure they can exist separately, but the two really work together to create a whole. Of course, put notes together willy-nilly and there's no guarantee of musicality. Same with wine. The food and pairing strategies below serve to help you find harmony in order to turn up the gastronomical stereo!

Red meat

Serve red wine. "Red wine with red meat" is one adage that rings true. Beef, lamb, and game are hearty. They're full-flavoured and heavy. They're packed with protein. Red wines—especially Cabernet Sauvignon, Malbec, Merlot, and Syrah—follow the same traits. Plus, hearty red wines tend to contain more tannins than other wines, and protein works wonders in smoothing out tannic wine.

Poultry

Serve fruity medium-bodied white wine. Everyone likes chicken, right? And nothing beats a holiday-festooned turkey. Similarly, most people are happy with dry medium-bodied white wine. We're talking Pinot Gris, Sémillon, and friends. If you want to get creative, try sparkling wine.

Pork

Serve medium to rich whites, light to medium reds. The "other" white meat can take to a lot of different wines. An off-dry Riesling goes gangbusters with roast pork (don't forget the applesauce), or if your wine choice swings red opt for a lighter rosso from Italy's Veneto region, or Gamay Noir in general. Ground pork stir-fried up with an Asian twist is a prime partner for exotic, aromatic Torrontés. The bottom line is that pork is highly wine-friendly; it really depends with how you sauce the swine.

Fish

With delicate fish serve light-to-medium white wine. The way you cook the fish makes all the difference. The delicacy of a poached fish needs a delicate wine like Pinot Blanc or Soave. If you're baking, seek a bit more texture from a white Bordeaux blend or Pinot Grigio. Frying in a glorious sea of butter? Open a Chardonnay or a sparkling wine. Overall a good strategy to follow is: the oilier the fish, the heavier the wine can be.

With firm fish serve medium white or light-to-medium red wine. Any fish that can be sold in "steaks" qualifies in this camp. For example, wild B.C. salmon has plenty of flavour, and it takes a wine with extra heft to get along with it. Likewise, halibut is no shrimp. White-wise, try both oaked or unoaked Chardonnays and Viognier. Red-wise, try a Pinot Noir. And don't forget rosé.

Shellfish

Serve light white wine. Look to fresh, crisp wines—just how you want your shellfish to be! Consider how lemon or lime are often employed with seafood to perk things up, then consider wines with comparably high acidity. It's also safe to bet on white wines with no, or neutral, oak flavour. Albariño, Chenin Blanc, and Riesling are bivalve and crustacean friendly. Sparkling wine is another refreshing, go-to option.

Vegetarian

Serve wine similar in flavour and texture to the veg. No offence to soy protein, but what's up with tofurkey and meatless meat substitutes? Vegetarianism and veganism are noble pursuits in their own right and can be celebrated as such (with wine). Vegetables, grains, legumes—all pair with vino. Simply consider flavours and texture. Earthy, hearty dishes featuring mushroom or eggplant go great with heartier, earthy reds. Lemon-splashed quinoa salad fares well with citrusy Sauvignon Blanc.

Spicy

Serve fruity, off-dry, and lower-alcohol white wine. Wine and spice can make strange bedfellows. Keep the capsaicin in relative check, and a slightly sweet, fruity wine like Gewürztraminer or an aromatic white blend will show through the spice. But if the food is heavy on jalapeño, go with beer.

Dessert

Serve red or white wine that's sweeter than the dessert. If the wine is too dry, the sweet dessert will make it seem even drier. And blander. Look for fortified wines like port and Marsala that are sweet but not cloying, or a lively and spritzy Moscato d'Asti to keep things light.

Oh, and a word about chocolate: it's harder to pair the cacao than you think. Stick to quality dark chocolate and still heed the advice to stay sweet with the wine. Grenache and sparkling Shiraz make interesting options, or for a different approach, try a fruit wine and drizzle a corresponding fruit sauce over the chocolate!

Cheese

Try anything. It won't hurt. A wine salesperson once said, "If you want to sell wine, serve cheese." Cheese makes everything taste good. Cheese is highly recommended before dinner, during dinner, and definitely after dinner. Creamy cheese is tasty with a creamy wine like white Rhône blends, harder aged cheese sings with a solid wine like Carmenère. And a beautiful match that never goes out of style is salty blue cheese and sweet Sauternes or late-harvest wine.

Food and Wine Pairing Tips

- Consider intensity. Big-flavoured wines tend to go with big-flavoured foods. What does "big-flavoured" mean? Full-bodied, fruit-forward wines you really feel in your mouth. The corollary is that light-flavoured wines tend to suit lighter dishes (the wildcard is sparkling wine, which seems to be able to go with just about any food thanks to its overtones of refreshment and celebration). This is the key reason why a robust Malbec runs roughshod over mixed greens, but goes amazing with a mixed grill.

- Either contrast or match food and wine flavours. A buttery Chardonnay matches a creamy alfredo sauce, and a meaty Cabernet matches, well, meat. On the other hand, a crisp and fruity Sauvignon Blanc works wonders in contrasting briny, rich oysters—and a fizzy, slightly sweet Lambrusco can tame a plate of fully loaded nachos.

- It's OK to play with your food. Just opened a Shiraz with an extra peppery kick? Try grinding a bit of black pepper on the dish to bridge the gap. Is that zesty Albariño overpowering the seafood? Squeeze a few drops of lemon juice on your fish to help things jive.

- Build flavour bridges. Can any wine go with any food? That's a stretch, but if your food is balanced in flavour you stack the odds in favour of a successful match. A steak or salmon on its own is a recipe for the doldrums, but a sprinkle of salt or a bit of lime will give the food some seasoned balance. A garden salad with a handful of roasted pine or pumpkin nuts (or bacon bits!) to flesh out an acidic vinaigrette will increase the wine-pairing potential.

- Keep things in perspective. Food and wine matches are moving targets. One night's perfect match may not prove as memorable the next day or week. Context and company also go with the wine and food.

Icon Maps

There is a wine for every meal, and there is a wine for every occasion. These icons will appear alongside each review to offer a few suggested food pairings and occasions to enjoy with every wine.

Food Icons

Beef — Big protein, whether it's roast, steak, or stew

Cheese — Hard or soft, stinky or mild

Dessert — Sweet, sticky, fruity, and fun!

Fish — Big or small, whole or fillet

Lamb — The other red meat

On Its Own — 'Nuff said

Pork — Chops, kebabs, loin—from nose to tail

Poultry — Turkey, chicken, duck, and any fowl

Shellfish — Bivalves and crustaceans

Vegetarian — Garden-approved and tofu-friendly

Occasions

BYO Crowd-pleasers; wines to pack along to the dinner party

Classic Wines that show good typicity; varietally true bottles

Patio/Picnic Sunshine in a bottle; sipping wines ready for alfresco dining

Rock Out Wines to let your hair down and crank it up to 11

Romance Wines to get busy with

Wednesday Wine Everyday bottles to get you through the mid-week hump

Wine Geek Eclectic wines outside the usual bottled domain

Winter Warmer Wines to ward off any chill

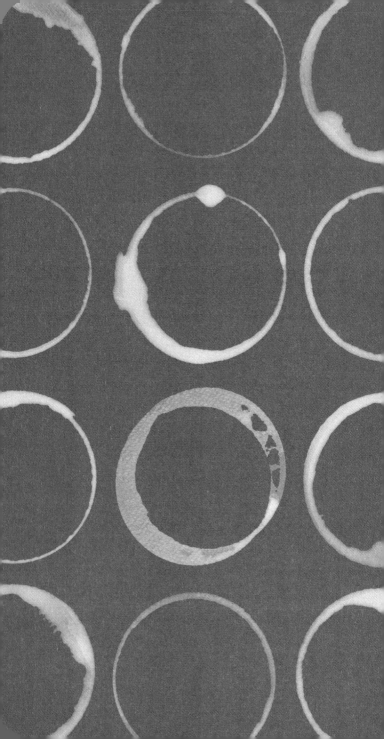

The Whites

Argentina

Finca Los Primos

2011 Torrontes
$9.98

Torrontés is one of those wines that make you smile as you sip. It's just plain fun to drink, thanks to the grape's penchant for producing fresh, enticingly aromatic white wines. So it's not really surprising that this Argentine grape is gaining global acclaim. (Oh, and one brief point of clarification: many wine labels ditch the accent over the *e* in Torrontés for simplification.) See for yourself with Finca Los Primos's Torrontés, a good introduction to the grape requiring minimal financial investment. It's super-fruity and super-fun, not as rich or overtly perfumed as some, but zingy and crisp and all-around easy sipping.

 Fried chicken

 Brie

Wednesday Wine, Winter Warmer

Portugal

Casal Garcia

N/V Vinho Verde
$10.99

They say you never get a second chance to make a first impression. Well, for a lasting first wine impression, serve Vinho Verde. It's pretty much the freshest wine around, with sharp acidity and a prickle of effervescence that certainly perks up the taste buds. Plus, at a mellow 10 percent alcohol level it's light enough to kick off the proceedings without worry of bogging down any palate. Serve it as a reception wine, serve it with the first course, or simply serve Vinho Verde all night long (ideally on a hot, humid night).

 Calamari

 Curried mussels

Patio/Picnic, BYO

Chile

Cono Sur

2011 Viognier
$10.99

Perhaps the perfect wedding wine? I know, I know, that's extremely difficult to qualify. However. Of the countless times I've been asked for "wedding wine" recommendations, 99 percent of the requests come with the stipulation that the wine must be cheap, crowd-pleasing, and food versatile. And year after year Cono Sur over-delivers with their pert Viognier. It's a joy to smell its lush, ripe tropical fruit backed by floral notes. And it's fun to swig thanks to the wine's overall balance and lively finish. In short, it has something for nearly everyone—including a budget-friendly price for whoever's footing the bill!

Chicken and pasta

Smoked salmon terrine

BYO, Wednesday Wine

Marani

N/V Mtsvane
$12.90

Forget the Old World, this bottle represents wine's Ancient World! Archaeological evidence points to modern-day Georgia as the birthplace of wine, in the fertile valleys of the South Caucasus some ten thousand years ago. Thankfully this sprightly little white tastes nothing like those rustic, resiny wines of yore. Made from the region's indigenous Mtsvane grape—which in Georgian means "new, young, and green"—the wine is full of apple and pear aromas melded to more savoury nuances of hay, honeysuckle, and wet slate, with a bright mid-palate leading to some white pepper spiciness on a short finish. This is a great choice to broaden your wine horizons.

 Spaghetti alle vongole

 Steamed Asian-style cod

Wine Geek, Patio/Picnic

 Argentina

Lurton

2012 Pinot Gris
$13.99

With apologies to Dos Equis, François Lurton may well be The Most Interesting Man in the Wine World. He's the original "flying winemaker," jetting across the globe to consult with wineries on six continents. He speaks (at least) three languages. And the dude races rally cars for fun (and even completed the Dakar Rally with a broken vertebrae)! But most importantly for our purposes, François Lurton is a champion for accessible, affordable wines. The Pinot Gris from his eponymous Argentina winery is a fine example. He was one of the first to plant the grape in Argentina, and it's proven a sage decision. It has all the fruit and freshness you could ask for in an everyday white, not to mention a satisfyingly rich texture and a smooth finish.

 Pho

Chicken fingers

Wednesday Wine, Classic

Argentina

Michel Torino

2011 CUMA Torrontés
$13.99

Springtime sipping wine
Mandarin rose in the glass
Moment please don't pass.

 On its own

 Chickpea and kale curry

Patio/Picnic, Wine Geek

7 790189 040074 >

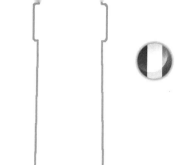

France

Ormarine

2010 Picpoul de Pinet
$13.99

This is 100 percent Picpoul from deep in the Coteaux du Languedoc. Peek what? Long where? Remember Rule #1 when hunting for great wine value: if the grape and/or region don't sound familiar, odds are you're in for a new taste treat! Piquepoul means "lip stinger" in French and is an homage to the grape's high acidity, and indeed the Ormarine is lively and light with good balance and a lemony kiss to finish. This is ocean-wise wine, perfect served with seafood—preferably from sustainably managed Ocean Wise sources!

 Fish stew

 Steamed clams

Wine Geek, Patio/Picnic

Italy

Mezzacorona

2011 Pinot Grigio
$14.49

Here we have a real piazza pounder. That is, a cheerful, refreshing, reasonably priced, and dangerously easy-drinking wine that pairs perfectly with alfresco imbibing. In my polite Canadian ways I had always referred to this style of wine as a "patio sipper." But then during casual conversation one hot, sunny day an American compatriot explained that stateside they refer to these wines as "porch pounders." That's certainly more assertive, not to mention alliterative. Chill this bottle down, find a piazza (or a porch or patio), and relish the wine's straight-up, fruity pear and lemony-fresh fun.

 On its own

 Dover sole

Patio/Picnic, Classic

8 004305 000088 >

Spain

Torres

2011 Viña Esmeralda
$14.49

Moscatel + Gewürztraminer = a noseful of goodness. Seriously, I don't think I'll ever grow tired of smelling this wine. It is aromatic to the nth degree, throwing off flower bouquets and baskets of tropical fruit—with a little orange peel tossed in for good measure. I might not bore of simply smelling Viña Esmeralda, but of course I will get thirsty, and thankfully this fragrant white goes down easy. There's evident sweetness, but it's nicely countered by brisk acidity. For best results, consume young for maximum freshness.

 Prosciutto-wrapped melon

 Crab and avocado salad

Wednesday Wine, BYO

Gehringer Brothers

2011 Classic Auxerrois
$14.99

Aux-*ahh*-what? It would be a shame to walk past this bottle simply because you don't recognize the grape. Auxerrois actually has quite a mysterious backstory, complete with grape doppelgängers and a handful of aliases. You'll find most Auxerrois in the Alsace region of France and Germany, but there are also modest plantings in B.C. Check out the Gehringer Brothers Classic Auxerrois for a great taste of the grape. It's full of nice stone fruit and flower blossoms, wrapped in an approachable, fruity-and-off-dry style that makes for fine everyday sipping.

 Seared scallops

 Bruschetta

Rock Out, Classic

France

Haut-Censy

2010 Muscadet Sèvre et Maine Sur Lie
$14.99

If it ain't broke, don't fix it.
Right? Muscadet with fresh
oysters is often cited as a perfect
pairing, and you know, there's
certainly nothing broken about
the match. While I wouldn't tout
Muscadet as the only option
with freshly shucked bivalves,
the typical crispness, citrus fruit,
and mineral (even briny)
qualities of good Muscadet do
go divinely with oysters. But
enough talk. Go rustle up some
Olympias or Kumamotos from
the fishmonger and grab a bottle
of the budget-savvy Haut-Censy,
which is bottled directly "on
lees" (sur lie)—that is, without
filtering—for maximum flavour
enjoyment.

 Oysters on the half shell

 Cajun snapper

Patio/Picnic, Classic

France

Louis Latour

2009 Ardèche Chardonnay
$14.99

Is this the Chardonnay that will lead us down the Middle Way? Admittedly, wine is not the path to spirituality (as much as people may feel enlightened while drinking it). Still, having endured overly oaked, caramel-bedecked Chardonnay confections, and then the polar opposite—devoid-of-character, blank-canvas unoaked Chards—the Ardèche comes across positively Goldilockian. It maintains crisp apple, lemon, and mineral tones but allows subtle oak spice and toast to permeate right on through to a pleasant, balanced finish. It's fresh yet oaky, rich but structured; it's just right.

 Macadamia-crusted snapper

 Smoked pork loin

Patio/Picnic, Romance

France

M. Chapoutier

2011 Bila-Haut Côtes du Roussillon
$14.99

"The rule of the game is to show we can make very interesting wines at very interesting prices." Over lunch in Vancouver recently Michel Chapoutier explained this was one of his main motivations. To do this he seeks out unique soils and terroir capable of expressing unique character. There's certainly no arguing with the price of this interesting white from sunny and stony Côtes du Roussillon. The Bila-Haut blanc blends together Grenache Blanc, Grenache Gris, and Macabeo in a lively white that folds citrus fruit with savoury notes of honeysuckle and almost a smoky note. It's fun, it's interesting, and it's great value.

 Tuna tartare

 Morbier

Wine Geek, Romance

Santa Rita

2011 Reserva Sauvignon Blanc
$14.99

"It don't mean a thang if it ain't got that twang." I saw this once on a pro-country-music tee. If I owned the shirt I'd wear it while sipping this SB, 'cuz it certainly has a twang that reverberates taste buds. Which is no small feat, mind you. It's a thin line between twang and underripe, acidic, tooth-enamel twinge. Santa Rita's Reserva Sauvignon Blanc has the requisite zippy gooseberry and passionfruit punch, but it's backed by great depth and a crisp, yet balanced, finish— remarkable given the price.

 Sweet-and-sour pork

 Shrimp scampi

Rock Out, Patio/Picnic

7 804330 221202 >

Chile

Emiliana

2011 Adobe Reserva Chardonnay
$15.00

Here's a wine for those who opine they can't afford to buy organic. Chile's Emiliana has worked hard to focus on 100 percent organic and biodynamic agriculture, and their entire range of wines reflects this care and commitment to both the land and the people who work the land. Adobe Reserva is their everyday line of wines, and the latest vintage of Chardonnay maintains super-value status. Sourced from Emiliana's cooler-climate vineyards in the Casablanca Valley, this lush white coats the tongue with sumptuous pineapple and crème brûlée before finishing big and warming. This is no wallflower; it's a bold, fruity, and lush Chard with certified green cred!

 Roast chicken

 Pasta alfredo

Winter Warmer, BYO

Boutari

2010 Moschofilero
$15.99

Hard to pronounce but easy to enjoy, Moschofilero (say mos-skoh-FEE-leh-roh) is Greece's indigenous aromatic grape. Boutari's Moscho is a perennial great value, offering a fruit bowl of cantaloupe, peach pit, and floral aromas in an overall fresh style that finishes citrusy and crisp. It's just a joy to drink: light-bodied but not too delicate. Also, checking in at a mellow 11.5 percent alcohol content, it makes a respectable lunchtime sipper.

On its own

Lemon-baked halibut

Wine Geek, Patio/Picnic

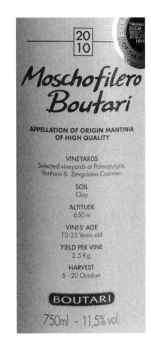

5 201022 574233 >

 Washington

Chateau Ste. Michelle

2010 Riesling
$15.99

Rieslings are the tube amps of the wine world. There's a warmth and purity to the fruit that's hard to match. When made well, Riesling has this richness balanced by a treble of acidity that simply makes for fantastic sipping. So crank up the volume and rock out to Chateau Ste. Michelle's Riesling, a perennial standby from the Columbia Valley that plays apple and lemon aromas off a smooth, just-off-dry core before finishing with a lick of crispness. Pair with Chinese takeout and your tuneage of choice.

 Spareribs

 Spring rolls

Rock Out, Wednesday Wine

Argentina

Crios de Susana Balbo

2011 Torrontés
$15.99

Impossibly floral with aromatics worthy of expletives, the Crios Torrontés is reminiscent of having your mouth washed out with soap—only in a wonderful way that's just for grown-ups. A cornucopia of scents await in this wine, from roses and tangerine rind to peach and lemon. It's a wine pick-me-up—an assertive, fresh, and fun dry white that is great for solo sipping. Or for a more adventurous pairing, try with tea-smoked duck or other smoked meats.

 On its own

 Chiu Chow goose

Classic, Romance

7 798068 480300 >

New Zealand

Two Tracks

2011 Sauvignon Blanc
$15.99

Well hello there, little bottle of sunshine. Thanks to its typical thirst-quenching acidity and fruity sensibility, zippy Sauvignon Blanc can brighten up any grey day. (It also works as refreshment on an already hot, sunny day!) Two Tracks captures this bright disposition perfectly. Made with grapes sourced from Sauv Blanc's holy land of Marlborough, it jumps out of the glass with melon, goose-berry, and cut grass before heeding to a plush mid-palate and lingering fresh and fruity finish. It's an easier drinking style of Sauvignon Blanc that aims to please.

 Oyster po' boy

 Cold tofu with scallions

BYO, Winter Warmer

Peter & Peter

2011 Zeller Riesling
$16.99

Did you read the back of cereal boxes when you were young? Well, reading wine labels is the adult equivalent. If you don't read the label you could be missing out. Take this Peter & Peter Zeller Riesling Feinherb aus der Steillage Qualitätswein Mosel. It might seem like a mouthful, but nothing a little Googling won't help decode: Peter & Peter is the wine name. Riesling is the varietal. Zeller is the village area the grapes come from, and Mosel, the region. Aus der Steillage indicates the steep slopes of the vineyards (a good thing). Feinherb tells us it's sweet. And Qualitätswein indicates a "quality wine." Phew! Or, just know that this is a lemon-PEZ-candy-fruity, tangy, and easy-drinking Riesling great for the patio.

 Pork schnitzel

 Angel food cake

Patio/Picnic, Wednesday Wine

QUINTA do AMEAL

2010

Branco Seco
Dry White Wine

ESTATE BOTTLED
PRODUZIDO ENGARRAFADO NA QUINTA
QUINTA DO AMEAL · SOC. AGR. S.A.
4990 - 787 REFOIOS DO LIMA · PONTE DE LIMA · PT
PRODUCE OF PORTUGAL

 Portugal

Quinta do Ameal

2010 Loureiro Vinho Verde
$16.99

Portugal continues to pleasantly surprise with some real wine gems. I'm not talking port, which has a long (and well-earned) reputation as one of the world's top fortified-wine categories. I'm referring to Portugal's whites and reds, which are arriving on wine shelves to showcase unique, indigenous grapes that bring new, exciting flavours. Wines like this Vinho Verde from Quinta do Ameal, which blows away the preconception that all Vinho Verde is light, simple, and spritzy. Made from organically grown Loureiro grapes, it tantalizes the taste buds with citrus, white flower, and an intense flint and wet stone mineral quality that builds as the wine warms in the glass.

 Clams and pork

 Grilled sardines

Wine Geek, Winter Warmer

British Columbia

Wild Goose

2011 Riesling
$16.99

Wild Goose is the little winery that could. From humble beginnings, Wild Goose has developed a serious reputation for producing top-notch B.C. wines, and they've maintained an endearing modesty through it all. During the late eighties, Wild Goose was one of the original proponents of "farm gate" wineries that make and directly sell their wine, and they continue to produce mouth-quenching, fruit-forward wines. Their latest Riesling doesn't sway from the course. Off-dry with bracing apple, apricot blossom, and notes of honey, it's a food-friendly white ready to slake your thirst and sate your locavore diet.

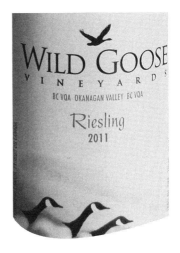

 Spot prawns

 Guanciale

BYO, Wednesday Wine

British Columbia

CedarCreek

2011 Riesling
$17.90

How do British Columbia's wines stack up to similar bottles from around the world? Pretty well, it turns out, at least for CedarCreek's tasty Riesling when it went head to head in a blind, brown-bag tasting attended by a slew of wine journalists and sommeliers. Against Rieslings from Germany and Australia, this homegrown bottle impressed with lemon-lime, apricot, and an overall rich but über-fresh style. The real kicker? CedarCreek's Riesling was the cheapest of the lot (the other two wines wouldn't qualify to be in these pages).

 On its own

 Clams casino

Wednesday Wine, Patio/Picnic

Blasted Church

2011 Hatfield's Fuse
$17.99

Honestly, I love pairing food and wine. They go together like ebony and ivory, like socks and shoes, like Henrik and Daniel. You know, in perfect harmony. And in this book, pains are taken to carefully consider appropriate dishes for each wine. However. Every once in a while there's a wine that just makes you want to pour a glass and sip it solo, alone with your thoughts. (Or maybe on a patio. With a friend.) Cue Hatfield's Fuse. Year after year this conspicuously aromatic white arrives to brighten our days with an orchard's worth of peach and citrus fruit followed by a zippy finish. Not that it doesn't go with food—in fact it's delicious with everything from takeout Thai to chicken fingers. If you're hungry.

On its own

Pad Thai noodles

Romance, BYO

Chile

Caliterra

2011 Tributo Sauvignon Blanc
$17.99

Ley. Da. You got me on my knees. Ley Da … The Leyda Valley stretching near Chile's coast has recently become an "it" wine growing sub-region, heralded for its "cool" cool-climate disposition that favours Chardonnay and Sauvignon Blanc. That's all well and good, but personally I can't think about the burgeoning region without having Eric Clapton's "Layla" run through my head. Get to know Leyda by sipping on Caliterra's Tributo Sauv Blanc, which is made from grapes harvested in the single Algarrobo vineyard near the city of Casablanca. It shows amazingly vibrant fruit see-sawed with a rich texture and fresh finish, a wine that nicely marries Sauvignon Blanc's fashionable fruit-forward exuberance with the grape's timeless elegance.

 On its own

Mussels gratin

Classic, Winter Warmer

8 31573 00027 8

De Martino

2011 Legado Reserva Chardonnay
$17.99

This is the George Clooney of Chardonnays. Does George Clooney even drink Chardonnay? I'm sure George Clooney drinks whatever the heck he wants, and no doubt he does it with style. That's the thing—this Chard is simply lively and full of character without trying too hard. Pear skin, citrus, and oak aromas (that's, like, probably Mr. Clooney's everyday cologne) lead to a rich, balanced mid-palate that finishes with a lingering spiciness. In short, it's an everyday wine carried with class.

 Steak at Chaya

 Chicken souvlaki

Wednesday Wine, Rock Out

Israel

Galil Mountain

2010 Viognier
$18.99

Boy oh boy, does this Viognier bear hug the palate. Certainly not in any mean-spirited manner—this ultra-lush white just oozes sumptuous fruit. It wafts out of the glass and coats the mouth with honey, apricot, pear, and rose petal. Then the toasty, well-integrated oak sidles up to the taste buds to add another layer of complexity. It would almost be too much plushness, but thankfully things are kept in check by enough tangy acidity and a spicy kick to finish.

On its own

Cream of corn soup

Wine Geek, Winter Warmer

Quails' Gate

2011 Chasselas–Pinot Blanc–
Pinot Gris
$18.99

You down with CPP?!? Yeah, you know me! The Chasselas–Pinot Blanc–Pinot Gris blend (or CPP for the acronym inclined) from Quails' Gate has become one of those classic patio poppers. It has everything you want in a warm-weather alfresco sipper: huge aromatics right out of the glass, buoyant stone fruit and citrus with a smidgen of sweetness so everything goes down easy, and a snappy finish. Of course, unlike white pants, these wine traits don't need to be exclusive to summer; the CPP is a year-round palate pick-me-up.

Halibut and chips

Fondue

Patio/Picnic, Wednesday Wine

St. Urbans-Hof

2010 Riesling
$18.99

The 2010 vintage was tough for German Riesling. Crop levels were down dramatically thanks to cold weather and ongoing rains during bud break, and harvesting had to wait till the late days of autumn. The increased hang time equated to increased sugar levels, but—bizarrely—higher acidity as well. However, the old saying goes that great winemakers can make great wine even in difficult years, and St. Urbans-Hof makes good on the adage with another classic Riesling. Rich and almost honeyed, it shows sumptuous applesauce and peach that's balanced by zippy acidity on a lingering finish.

 Crab cakes

 Tonkotsu ramen

Classic, Romance

Australia

Tahbilk

2010 Marsanne
$18.99

Have you ever felt out of place?
Like you've gotten off the New York subway at 110th Street in Spanish Harlem and suddenly find yourself wondering how many blocks it is to Central Park? Marsanne is certainly not the top grape associated with Australia. It's not even in the top ten. And it's certainly a long way from the northern Rhône Valley to Nagambie Lakes, Tahbilk's home turf. Yet there it is every year, another sumptuous Aussie white made 100 percent from Marsanne, a grape the winery first planted in the 1860s! Fresh lemon, peach pit, and honey continually make this a classic Marsanne, a welcome stranger perhaps and certainly a quick friend at the dinner table.

 Roast pork tenderloin

 Fried plantain

Classic, Wine Geek

9 312163 100079 >

New Zealand

Villa Maria

2011 Private Bin Sauvignon Blanc
$18.99

Considering how the "Kiwi style" has come to define what Sauvignon Blanc should taste like, you'd be forgiven for thinking New Zealand has a long history with wine. In fact most of the country's vineyards and wineries are still young, many established in the mid-1980s. This gives Villa Maria Estate true pioneer status, as the family-owned winery celebrated 50 years of production with their 2011 vintage. In reflecting back, founder Sir George Fistonich claims "There have only been three days over the last 50 years that I have not drunk wine." Given the consistency of their consistently good Private Bin Sauvignon Blanc—with its textbook grapefruit and gooseberry, slight herbaceous qualities, and surprising richness that finishes tangy and dry—it's easy to see why.

 On its own

 Crab cakes

Classic, Patio/Picnic

Wither Hills

2011 Pinot Gris
$18.99

You can just picture Pinot Gris screaming, "Don't pigeonhole me!" Like the newest indie band, Pinot Gris may at times struggle to define itself, but there's no denying PG has many unique styles. Fruity B.C. Gris? Check. Oily Alsace Gris? Oui. Light and crisp Grigio? Si. Robust, subtly sweet Gris? Sweet as! New Zealand Pinot Gris is charting a style all its own, typically rich and fruity and slightly off-dry. See for yourself with Wither Hill's exuberant Gris, which has tons of pear and flower aromas, an amazing overall intensity, and a zippy yet sweet finish.

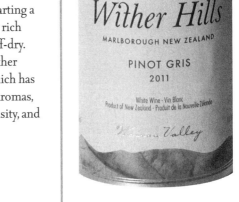

 Smoked trout

Smoked tofu

Wine Geek, Winter Warmer

Italy

Beni di Batasiolo

2011 Gavi di Gavi Granée
$19.99

This is the real deal. One hundred percent Cortese di Gavi, or Gavi di Gavi, or simply darn fine drinking wine. From the northwestern reaches of the Piedmont region of northern Italy, this white is elegant yet lusty, and delicate yet intense. Apologies if that sounds a little too romantic, but this is a precious bottle from the get-go. Wet rock and rose petal aromas linger with lemon pith, leading into a tart burst of a finish. All this and the bottle is plain classy. Pour this Gavi on your next date night and watch the tension melt away.

 Oysters

 Hainan chicken

Wine Geek, Romance

France

Domaine de Vaugondy

2010 Vouvray
$19.99

Chenin Blanc is a real Renaissance grape. (Actually, from a historical perspective it far predates the Renaissance period.) You'll find shining examples of Chenin Blanc in styles ranging from bone dry to dessert-sweet, not to mention as sparkling and fortified wines. In the Loire Valley, which is regarded as Chenin's pre-eminent region (and where the grape is also known as *Pineau de la Loire*), you'll find all the above. The Domaine de Vaugondy hails from the designated, Chenin-centric appellation of Vouvray. It has intense flavours that dance across the tongue, delighting in refreshment from zingy fruit and flower blossom aromas to a tangy, well-balanced citrus finish.

 Black cod

 Lentil dhal

Wine Geek, Patio/Picnic

3 760078 211087 >

Forrest

2010 The Doctors' Riesling
$19.99

Have you tried a Riesling from New Zealand? New Zealand is no Sauvignon Blanc mono-culture. Heck, even in this year's *Had a Glass* we have a Pinot Gris and Riesling joining the requisite SB, and there would be a Pinot Noir as well if most weren't above the $20 mark. The Doctors' Riesling is simply delish, fruity with lime and baked apple, not to mention a mellow sipper thanks to supple balance. The wine's 8.5 percent alcohol level points to its overall sweetness, but it is anything but cloying thanks to lip-smacking acidity. This is a great option when you're ready to get off the beaten Marlborough path!

 Duck curry

 Goat cheese and fresh berries

Wine Geek, Romance

France

Hugel et Fils

2010 Gentil "Hugel"
$19.99

What is "classic"? A three-button suit? A little black dress? A handwritten thank-you note? I don't know anymore, but I do know that it matters. Sure, you could text a thank you, but is it really the same? Show up at your next dinner party with a bottle of Hugel Gentil and no one can deny that you care. It's a classic white, and classy for it. In the ancient Alsace tradition, the Gentil blends a five-grape medley of Gewürztraminer, Pinot Gris, Riesling, Muscat, and Sylvaner into an amazingly balanced, highly quaffable potable that is elegant, timeless, and tasty.

Pulled pork tacos

Onion tart

Classic, Winter Warmer

Mission Hill

2010 Reserve Chardonnay
$19.99

There is a lot going on in this Chardonnay. Personally I'm not big on laundry-list wine reviews that spew out innumerable adjectives in seemingly descriptive one-upmanship. But seriously, I noted pear, apricot, pineapple, baking bread, oak, vanilla, baking spice . . . and those were just aromas! Then you taste the wine and it's plush and rich, yet spicy and fresh. To the point, it's simply darn tasty and complex thanks to great fruit and partial barrel fermentation followed by seven-month sur lie aging. More to the point, it's a good drop.

 Orange chicken

 Orange-marinated carnitas

Wednesday Wine, Winter Warmer

Notes

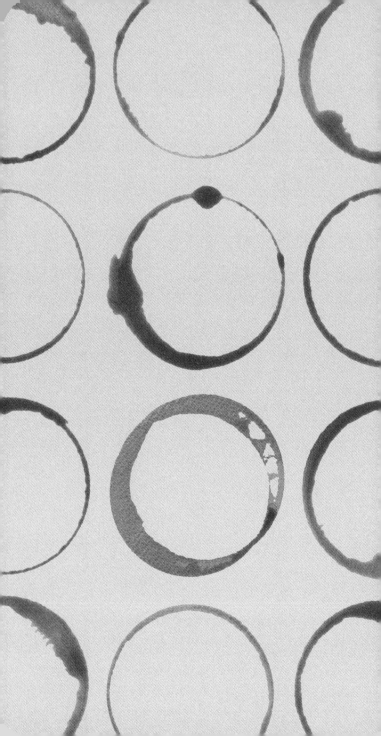

The Pinks

Portugal

Mateus

N/V Rosé
$9.99 (or $18.99 for 1.5 L)

There's nothing like the good ol' days. You know, when Mateus rosé came in a flask-shaped bottle, the Four Tops reigned over the radio dial, and the evenings were long and filled with leisurely whisperings of sweet nothings on the porch. Oh, wait. Mateus still comes in a flagon, Mayer Hawthorne is soulfully crooning on the iPod, and this nostalgia wine—brimming with comfort—is still cheap enough for porch pounding. Slightly frizzante and strawberry-licious, obviously sweet but nowhere near cloying, this wine is serious fun.

 Fried chicken

 Sausages

Patio/Picnic, Rock Out

Argentina

Altosur

2011 Malbec Rosé
$13.99

This wine is bewitching in the glass. A vibrant dark pink that sparkles when the sunlight catches it so; if you put it on a chip at Benjamin Moore and called it "nouveau blush" it would jump off the shelves and onto parlour walls. Of course it's more than a pretty colour; this is seriously rich rosé made from high-altitude-grown Malbec grapes. It's replete with candied cherry and herbs, and just like red wines made from Malbec goes great with backyard BBQs.

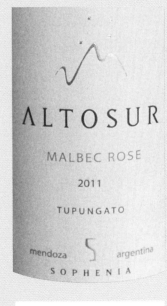

 Rib-eye

 Grilled loin chops

Winter Warmer, Wednesday Wine

France

Gassier

2011 Sables d'Azur Côtes de Provence Rosé
$15.99

There's nothing like a little skin contact. It is, after all, what gives rosé wine its seductive blush. Crush red grapes and leave the skins in contact with the juice for 6, 12, even 36 hours (it's the winemaker's decision) before siphoning off and you're left with bewitching shades ranging from onion skin to hot pink. Provence's classic Sables d'Azur leans to the former. This blend of Grenache, Syrah, and Cinsault pours a fetching salmon-pink in the glass and reveals exciting berry and lemon on first whiff. Rich but fresh through and through, it finishes thoroughly dry and epitomizes patio quaffer!

 Grilled salmon

 Turkey burgers

Patio/Picnic, Classic

British Columbia

Road 13

2011 Honest John's Rosé
$15.99

Road 13 says this is a "red wine lover's rosé." I really like the sentiment. It nicely captures one of rosé's advantages: fresh enough for a patio, but rich enough for a hearty, protein-heavy meal. Pink wine offers the best of both white and red wines! The latest vintage of this perennial good-value quaffer positively bursts with berry, has a nice little lick of spice, and finishes crisp and dry. A swamp mix of Pinot Noir, Gamay, and Merlot with a smattering of other grapes (Viognier, Syrah, Malbec, Rousanne, Chenin Blanc), the singular end result is one crowd-pleasing rosé.

Grilled halibut

Arancini

BYO, Romance

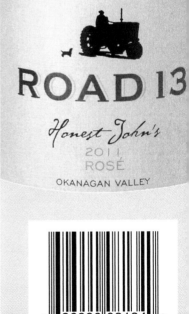

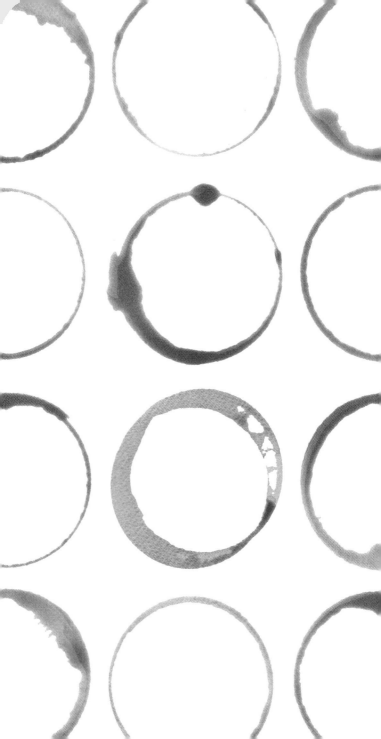

The Reds

 Italy

Benvenuto

2009 Barbera
$7.99

First things first: this is not your northern Italian Barbera. The grape's name is the same, but we're talking completely different cultivars. This is Barbera del Sannio, the Barbera of the south. Confused? You won't be when you taste this bottle. It packs a lot of punch for under ten bucks! Exciting black cherry, licorice, and floral aromatics kick things off and segue to a juicy, robust texture that builds to a gutsy finish with firm tannins. Translation: This is your new everyday red that works just as well with Wednesday pizza as it does with the weekend BBQ.

 Pizza funghi

 Burgers

Wednesday Wine, Rock Out

Bodegas Piqueras

2010 Marques de Rojas
$9.99

An interesting 2008 study of wine drinkers didn't find much of a correlation between price and happiness. In other words, just because a wine cost more didn't mean that tasters would enjoy it more. In fact, on average they preferred the less expensive wines! The study concludes by acknowledging that "both the prices of wines and wine recommendations by experts may be poor guides for non-expert wine consumers." Look, I don't want to lose my job, but I do want to remind you that great wine is relative (and subjective). You'll likely be pleased as punch sipping on this ten-buck Spanish Garnacha, which is rich and spicy, and a darn good buy.

 Meatloaf

 Turkey and Swiss on rye

BYO, Winter Warmer

8 414837 010545 >

Italy

Paiara

2009 Rosso
$9.99

"Plum and nettle" sounds like a good name for a boutique produce store. They're actually the first two sensations that jumped to mind when I stuck my nose into the wineglass. Paiara is a cheerful red from Puglia, the limits of southern Italy where the Negroamaro grape reigns supreme. You'll find it in this bottle along with Cabernet Sauvignon, and the two cultivars come together to create a robust wine with dark fruit and whiffs of floral and herb that finishes gutsy and just a tad rustic. All in all it's a smart little wine buy.

PAIARA

PUGLIA
INDICAZIONE GEOGRAFICA TIPICA
2009

 Eggplant parmigiana

 Meatballs

Winter Warmer, Patio/Picnic

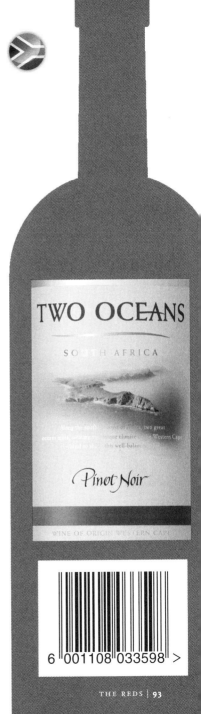

Two Oceans

2011 Pinot Noir
$10.99

Don't confuse being thrifty with being cheap. In fact, as headlines remain overrun with talk of "belt tightenings" and "austerity measures," spendthrift ways seem so gauche. Admittedly, Pinot Noir is not the first grape that rolls to mind when considering value-priced wines. But the Two Oceans Pinot breaks the stereotype. True, this bottle won't get confused with Grand Cru Burgundy, but it offers lots of cherry and char flavour for the price. And thanks to its lightweight freshness and modest alcohol level it makes for a great table red.

 Mushroom quiche

 Thai basil beef

Wednesday Wine, Patio/Picnic

 Argentina

Finca Los Primos

2011 Malbec
$11.97

This bottle still has it. True, it continues to inch up in price (when it first appeared in *Had a Glass* it sold for $9.99!), but it still over-delivers for an everyday red. Actually, the back label sums things up nicely: "An easy drinking, straight up Malbec." Enough said. You won't sit around contemplating this Malbec's plush blackberry fruit and whiff of vanilla and toasty oak, but you'll certainly be content cracking it open after a day at the office to pair with a quick meal.

Frozen vegetarian pizza

Burgers

BYO, Winter Warmer

Portugal

Cortello

2008 Touriga Nacional
$11.99

This is the Simon Cowell of wines! Smooth and soothing at first but acerbic and fresh to end, Cortello brings plush berry, plum, and spice while building to a lip-puckering end. Which is more than most eleven-buck bottles offer, and further proof that an "x" factor for finding great value wines is to seek out lesser-known grapes. In this case its Touriga Nacional—a workaday Portuguese grape common in the country's fortified port and robust reds, but little known outside the country.

 Linguiça sausage

 Kofta

Rock Out, Wine Geek

 Spain

Anciano

2003 Gran Reserva Tempranillo
$12.99

The grapes used to make this wine were picked in 2003! Think about that. A lot has happened in the subsequent years. And while the world went about its business this wine sat deep in the cellars in sun-drenched Valdepeñas. Waiting. And waiting. Opened now, the wine still smells fruity and fresh, with lots of black cherry and vanilla. It's still grippy and spicy on the finish, but nicely mel-lowed in the mid-palate. Bottom line: At $12.99 this bottle offers an enjoyable, accessible look at how a wine changes as it ages. For that alone it will impress your wine friends, and the fact that it comes wrapped in a cool old-school wire cage is a total aesthetic bonus.

 Pork pibil

 Moussaka

Romance, Wine Geek

Antaño

2008 Rioja Crianza
$12.99

Here's a perfect introduction to Spain's famed Rioja wine region. It's an honest example of Tempranillo, which is Rioja's star cultivar, at an honest price. Actually this lively wine blends Tempranillo with a little Garnacha, Graciano, and Mazuelo grapes—common practice in Rioja. Then, following Spanish regulation, this Crianza-designated wine ages for at least two years (one of which must be in oak). The final wine is a straightforward red with cherry fruit, earthiness, toasty oak, and vanilla that finishes with a tickle of spiciness.

  Jamón Ibérico

Tomato tart

Classic, Wednesday Wine

Argentina

Argento

2010 Reserva Bonarda
$12.99

No doubt about it, Malbec has become the go-to Argentine red. The appeal is understandable, but have you considered how this move to Malbec might make Bonarda feel? A generation ago Bonarda was the most widely planted grape in Argentina, the main cultivar that surely motivated many a tango. Today it's largely ignored for its A-list cousin. Bonarda might not have the legs or the depth of Malbec, but that's part of its value proposition. Typically juicy, punchy, and fresh, Bonarda aims to please in a pleasant everyday style. Check out Argento's Reserva Bonarda for a first-hand taste. A shocking ruby-purple colour in the glass and chock full of red fruit, flowers, and vanilla, it's a real charmer for the price.

 Pepperoni pizza

 Beef tacos

Wednesday Wine, Patio/Picnic

Australia

McLarens on the Lake

2009 Cabernet Sauvignon
$13.00

The label explains that the grapes for this Cabernet Sauvignon were grown in the winery's Communication Road Vineyard near Maslin's Beach in the seaside region of McLaren Vale. McLaren Vale is one of Australia's prettiest wine areas (not to mention it's home to one of the best wine events going, the Sea & Vines Food & Wine Festival held annually in June). Apparently Maslin's Beach is one of Australia's prime nude beaches (I can vouch for the merits of the wine festival, but not the beach!). Perhaps the views and laid-back beach vibe inspire the mulberry, menthol, and overall vivacious lusciousness in this bottle, which has everything you could ask for in a nicely priced, fruit-forward Cab.

 Pulled pork

 Beef burritos

BYO, Romance

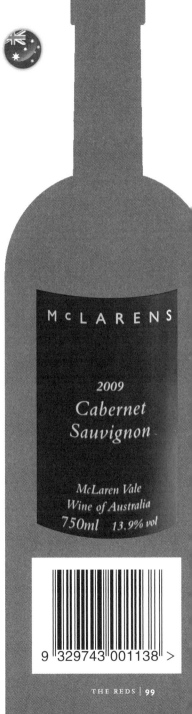

British Columbia

Averill Creek

2009 Prevost
$13.99

Averill Creek is proudly Island wine. The front of the label clearly states "Estate Grown Vancouver Island," and the winery has 40 acres to its name in the beautiful Cowichan Valley. This Island wine is also proudly unique, and we're better off for it. Prevost is a blend of mostly Marechal Foch with a dollop of Cabernet Sauvignon and Merlot. The unusual blend is a breath of fresh air, and this vibrant red comes across like a walk through the forest after a summer rain, full of ripe black fruit with a whiff of vegetation, herbs, and wood. At a reasonable 12.6 percent alcohol this is also no slouch of a bottle; it finishes dry and tart and screams to be paired with BBQ or roasts.

 Roast lamb

 Flank steak

Winter Warmer, Rock Out

Italy

Branciforti

2010 Nero d'Avola
$13.99

Is Nero d'Avola the new Malbec? Actually no, and there's no need to attempt a comparison. But if you're looking for a new punchy red in your life it's worth checking out Sicily's star red grape. Start with Branciforti's Nero. Brooding with spice and earth, this robust red exudes the warmth and richness of the southern Italian isle it calls home—then it wakes you from any wine daydreaming with an intense, fairly tannic finish.

 Grilled pork chops

 Lamb stew

Classic, Wednesday Wine

Spain

Laya

2009 Almansa
$13.99

It's important to have a meatloaf wine. Certain days just call for meatloaf (they tend to coincide with a forecast for cold and grey). And meatloaf calls for meatloaf wine. Actually, I'll take meatloaf any time of the year. I'll even enjoy "meatless" meatloaf if vegetarian cuisine is on the menu. Easy to make, even better in a sandwich the next day, meatloaf is ideal comfort food. And its heartiness goes great with a rich, smooth red like Laya. From the Almansa region in southern Spain, Laya is a blend of Garnacha and Monastrell grapes, showing lots of dark berry fruit and vanilla backed by a smoky, toasty oak finish. All in a classy package that belies the wine's $14 price tag.

 Meatloaf

 Quinoa loaf

Winter Warmer, BYO

South Africa

Roodeberg

2010 Red
$13.99

Remember when "cyber" was the prefix du jour? Like cybercafés, which were cafés you could go to and spend $8 an hour to surf the Internet (which itself was pretty cyberrifically known as the "information superhighway"). If you happened to hit a cybercafé while backpacking around Europe in the 90s, you were probably lucky enough to even order a glass of wine while checking your Hotmail account! Anyways, I first started drinking Roodeberg in the cyber-heyday, and you know, the wine still has it going on. Just juicy berry and cassis with mellow oak and a fresh, balanced finish—the sort of everyday red weekday meals were made for.

 Tex-Mex tacos

 Duck lettuce wraps

Wednesday Wine, Romance

 South Africa

Six Hats

2010 Shiraz
$13.99

You buy fair trade bananas, coffee, and chocolate, so why not buy fair trade wine? The six hats behind this Shiraz represent the six principles behind the wine (partnership, change, potential, equity, dignity, and sustainability), and the winery's commitment to fair trade is motivated by their desire to include people as part of a wine's "terroir." It's a worthy—and thankfully tasty—endeavour, full of good ambition and juicy cassis, intriguing soy-sauce aromas, and a peppery kick to end.

 Burgers

Baby back ribs

BYO, Patio/Picnic

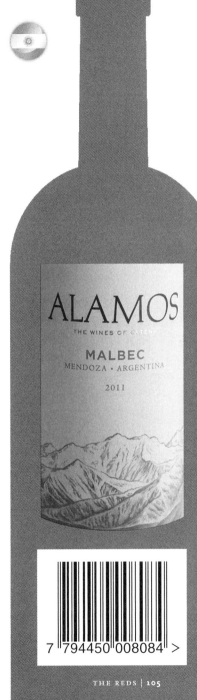

Argentina

Alamos

2011 Malbec
$14.99

Man, what I wouldn't give to be tucking into an ojo de bife at La Cabrera in Buenos Aires right now. Best. Steak. Ever. Of course I'll admit this claim could be contentious. I'll allow that Argentina is full of fantastic steakhouses. And I realize that I can cry all I want for Argentina but that rib-eye is still ten thousand kilometres away. So I'll resign myself to opening a classic Argentine Malbec like this Alamos, inhale its cherry and violet perfume, toss on some Carlos Gardel, ready the charcoal in the comfort in my abode, and cook up a rib-eye to match this meaty, gutsy red. Second. Best. Steak. Ever.

 Rib-eye

 Any other cut

Wednesday Wine, Winter Warmer

Castillo de Maluenda

2009 Punto y Coma Garnacha
$14.99

Suppose it was only a matter of time. This wine basically has an emoticon across its label. Just add a parenthesis and you have a winking eye ;). Punto y coma actually means "semicolon" in Spanish. It's all cute, and kind of funny considering the vines that produced the grapes for this wine way predate the Internet. Forty-year-old Garnacha vines to be exact, from the sunny climes of Calatayud in Zaragoza Province. The label may nearly wink but the wine is all business: black cherry, dusty earth, and mineral, with a lashing of spiciness to end. Text your friends, it's time to BBQ ;)

 Maui ribs

 Cabrales

Patio/Picnic, Wine Geek

South Africa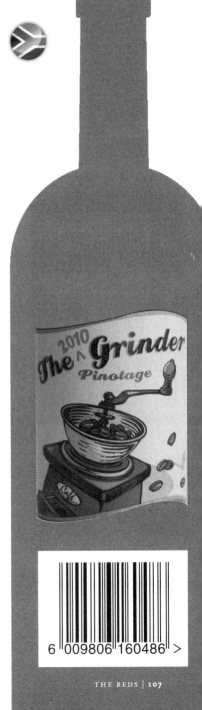

The Grinder

2010 Pinotage
$14.99

Full disclosure: This is not the style of wine I personally gravitate toward. It's a little over the top. But then that comes as no surprise considering the wine is called "The Grinder" and has a highly graphic, highly colourful label sporting a coffee grinder. The thing is, every time I pour this wine for friends or family their eyes light up. People love this wine. A crazy potpourri of roast coffee bean, chocolate, and smoked meat front this plush, fruity, and smooth red. It's an easy-drinking Pinotage that screams FUN!

 Chili

 Soy sauce chicken

BYO, Wednesday Wine

Chile

Montes

2010 Classic Series Cabernet Sauvignon
$14.99

A lot of wines out there need to work on their core. They look pretty and all that with their pert labels on the wine shelves. And many impress right out the blocks with enticing aromas. But then they get all flabby around the midpoint, just plump fruit and oak with no structure or acidity to firm things up. Not Montes's Classic Cab Sauv. It's built for speed and strength, plush yet zippy, with rich plum, caramel, and smoky oak backed by a lean structure and a bold finish that shows great stamina.

 Steak tartare

 Chipotle-braised lamb

Classic, BYO

Chile

Viña Maipo

2010 Reserva Carmenere
$14.99

Looking to let a new grape into your wine life? Might I suggest Carmenère (you'll also find it spelled Carménère or simply Carmenere), which should chart right at the top for BBQ red. Kind of like a savoury Merlot with attitude, Carmenère is often described as earthy, herby, and peppery. For a great introduction, fire up the grill and check out Viña Maipo's approachable Carmenère, with its rich, ripe plum and currant fruit backed by jalapeño and a slightly bitter finish.

 Beef kebabs

 Grilled leg of lamb

Patio/Picnic, Wine Geek

Chile

Bisquertt

2010 La Joya Reserve Merlot
$15.99

Remember when radio-friendly R & B ruled the airwaves? You know, late 80s through mid-90s, when funny-spelled and single-worded band names, choreographed clothes, and dance moves were da bomb. Boyz II Men. Jodeci. Guy. It was all feel-good, heartfelt emotions worn on a silk polka-dot shirt sleeve. Smooth without being raunchy. Full of flava. Well, La Joya is R & B Merlot, and enjoying its plush, ripe black-berry and soft-yet-fresh vanilla finish, I couldn't help but New Jack Swing.

 Speck

 Philly cheesesteak

Rock Out, Winter Warmer

Boutari

2008 Naoussa
$15.99

Fear not, this wine is foodie friendly! Actually, can we come up with a better term than "foodie"—I mean, I'm into food and knowing where my food comes from and all that. But I'd never call myself a foodie. It has the same patina as hipster. Who wants to be labelled a hipster? Anyways, if you care about pairing food and wine you should be looking for refreshing reds like this Naoussa, a cool bottle from northern Greece made with the Xinomavro grape. It trades rich and extracted for punchy and savoury, making it super-versatile in the kitchen and ready to take on everything from big protein to creamy sauces.

 Cuban sandwich

 Lamb souvlaki

Wine Geek, Wednesday Wine

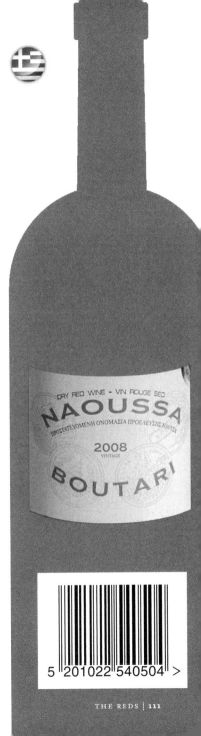

Paul Mas Estate

2011 Single Vineyard Collection Malbec
$15.99

Think all Malbec comes from Argentina? Malbec's modern story may be in South America, but the grape's history is in France. Paul Mas seems intent on reclaiming Malbec cred for La Belle Pays with its delightfully lush and velvety rendition sourced from Le Gardemiel, a vineyard in southern France located some 200 kilometres from Malbec's alleged birthplace of Cahors. It's enticingly aromatic, with ripe dark fruit and a balanced, plush finish, and makes for great uncorking any day of the week.

 Rack of lamb

 Aged cheddar

Wednesday Wine, Romance

Italy

Ricossa

2010 Barbera d'Asti
$15.99

This is a classic cool-climate gateway bottle. If you typically drink Zinfandel or Shiraz, your first sip of Barbera d'Asti may come across like a wine curveball. Hailing from the cooler reaches of northern Italy where Barbera grapes bathe in fog-drenched hills, the Ricossa swaps ripe dark fruit for tangy raspberry—not to mention floral notes and an underlying earthiness. It trades richness for zippiness, maintaining good overall balance that helps make the wine immensely food-friendly.

 Roast pork tenderloin

 Roast turkey

Classic, BYO

Australia

Yering Station

2010 Little Yering Pinot Noir
$15.99

Nothing lasts, nothing is finished, and nothing is perfect. In essence this is the spirit of *wabi-sabi*, and though it might sound mournful at first, there's real beauty in seizing the moment and letting life be. While your glass is full of Little Yering Pinot Noir, all will seem perfect. Bright cherry and berry fruit melts into more savoury toasty oak, tobacco, and vanilla. Finished? Simply remember that you can always buy another bottle. Nothing may last, but nothing is finished!

 Crispy squab

Mushroom ravioli

Winter Warmer, Wednesday Wine

Campo Viejo

2008 Rioja Crianza
$16.99

This wine is like a sauna for your tongue. It's classic Rioja with a modern bent, full of rich cherry fruit complemented by classic toasted wood and cedar qualities from the Crianza-mandated twelve months in barrel. A bold, grippy finish highlights undulating plum and toasted wood, and to maximize the wine sauna experience it's recommended to alternate sips of this Rioja with ice water.

 Lamb tagine

 Manchego

Patio/Picnic, Rock Out

Italy

Colle Secco

2008 Rubino Montepulciano d'Abruzzo
$16.99

Pretty but brawny. Turns out this can be quite the winning combination for a wine. Colle Secco's Rubino first entices with its gorgeous, inky purple-black colour. Then on first sip you're hit with plush, rich plum fruit and an underlying base of savoury herbs and hot asphalt that calls to mind the sun-baked hills of Abruzzo that are home to this wine's vineyards. But this full-bodied red is not afraid to slap the taste buds, and it ends balanced but grippy, and with a lasting sensation that will make you want to lick your lips.

 Pecorino Pepato

 Bresaola

Classic, Romance

Uruguay

Don Pascual

2009 Reserve Tannat
$16.99

Some wines shout. Other wines whisper. They can both be great, as long as the bottle has something to say. But there is something really captivating about a wine that lures you in with a firm but plaintive warble, kind of like Kurt Wagner in a Lambchop song. Don Pascual's Reserve Tannat is bold but firm, strong without being extroverted. Blackberry, fig, and anise shine through and lead to a dry, grippy finish. Give this wine time, put *What Another Man Spills* on repeat, break out a decanter, and let things exhale throughout the night. (Oh, and in case you didn't notice, this wine is from Uruguay. Not an everyday find, and certain to appeal to wine fanboys.)

 Lamb kebabs

 Oka

Wine Geek, Winter Warmer

Italy

Illuminati

2010 Riparosso Montepulciano d'Abruzzo $16.99

The Riparosso is a velour suit for the taste buds. It's also a tongue twirler of a name. But most importantly, it's a perfect transition wine. True, it will pour just fine all seasons of the year, but come spring (or fall), when I like to ease my palate away from (or toward) heavily oaked and tannic reds, this is the call. Made from 100 percent Montepulciano grapes from Italy's Abruzzo region, this lively red sees eight months aging in Slovenian oak, but the barrels are massive 2,500-litre affairs that impart little flavour. Showing black cherry fruit and engaging baked earth and spice, the Riparosso is smooth throughout with a nicely balanced, lip-smacking finish. It pairs up wonderfully with one-pot wonders like chili or stew.

Gratin Dauphinois

Beef stew

Classic, Patio/Picnic

Jacob's Creek

2009 Reserve Cabernet Sauvignon
$16.99

Classy Coonawarra Cabernet.
Say that ten times fast! There's
something simply romantic
about Coonawarra, from the way
it rolls off the tongue to its
renowned *terra rossa* soils,
streaked with red clay, that lend
themselves to one of the world's
unique terroirs. Though other
grapes grow well in this remote
pocket of South Australia,
Cabernet Sauvignon steals most
of the glory in Coonawarra. Try
Jacob's Creek Reserve Cabernet
Sauvignon to taste why. Classic
eucalypt (think minty or
menthol) mixed with mulberry
and a sprinkle of earth, this is a
rich red that is quite strong and
bold overall, and ends with a
grippy, lingering finish.

 Lamb shoulder roast

 Portobello burgers

Classic, Patio/Picnic

Austria

Zvy-Gelt

2009 Zweigelt
$16.99

Acidity in wine is like baking with salt. I mean, caramels are great. But salted caramels really make the taste buds sing! This is particularly true for red wines, which are more likely to undergo malolactic fermentation and often become overly plush and smooth. Acidity in wine actually enhances the fruit, and it can complement food pairings as well. Which is why a grape like Zweigelt, which has naturally higher acidity, comes across so fun and food-friendly! The bold-labelled Zvy-Gelt is all velvety cherry and spice, with a light and refreshing structure overall.

 Roast squab

 Felafel

Wine Geek, Winter Warmer

Portugal

Borges

2007 Quinta de São Simão da Aguieira
$17.99

This is Valentine's Day wine. Or, why wait? This Portuguese red will create romance any day of the year. The hot-pink label sets the mood, and the lively wine inside the bottle will get tongues tied—if they're not already from trying to say the names of the indigenous grapes that comprise the wine's blend: Touriga Nacional, Tinta Roriz, and Trincadeira. It comes together with intriguing aromas of plum, violet, leather, and watermelon backed by a punchy, nicely balanced finish. Pair it up with a cheese plate and charcuterie platter and you've created a great reason to stay in.

 Salami

 Serra da Estrela

Romance, Patio/Picnic

Australia

Chapel Hill

2010 Parson's Nose Shiraz
$17.99

Finally, I've found a wine to pair with "Suite: Judy Blue Eyes"! Crank on the Crosby, Stills & Nash while uncracking the screw cap on this Shiraz, and this epic jam will come alive in experiential stereo. Rich, ripe aromas of plum, blueberry, and toasty oak spice kick things off with a pretty pop start. But then a bold, powerful structure rumbles through the wine and sets a hearty pace until, almost five minutes in, things pick up with spice and oak—which builds until the toe-curling finish breaks at 6:34 with an exotic, black-pepper crescendo!

 Lamb burgers

Beef Wellington

Rock Out, Winter Warmer

8 50297 00019 7

France

Maison des Bulliats

2010 Régnié
$17.99

"The first vines of Régnié were planted by Reginus, a Roman nobleman and romantic," **explains the back label.** There you have it: Régnié is for lovers. It also happens to be the newest of the ten Beaujolais Crus, the designated sub-regions of southern Burgundy that truly highlight the beautiful tastiness of the Gamay grape (and make Beaujolais Nouveau seem like soda pop). This is about as cheap as Cru Beaujolais gets, and if you're curious it's worth every penny. Aromatic with berry fruit and floral notes, this is a bright, fruity red with an engaging bramble and mineral foundation. It finishes fresh and on the lighter side, and is super-food-friendly.

 Carrot ginger soup

 Duck confit

Classic, Wednesday Wine

California

Matchbook

2009 Syrah
$17.99

"Blended for Greater Flavor." I love that this claim is laid out on the bottle's back label. It's true! Blending can add great flavour, and in this Cali standby it's responsible for bright berry and cherry cola, lots of plushness, and a hit of Syrah-supplied pepper spice to end. Granted, the front of the label simply labels the wine as Syrah, but considering things check in at 91% Syrah and 9% Cabernet Sauvignon, to call this wine blended is completely legit. (In California a wine can be labelled as a varietal as long as it contains at least 75% of the grape.)

Shepherd's pie

Vegetarian lasagna

Rock out, Romance

California

Cline

2010 Zinfandel
$18.99

This Zinfandel is the luxury SUV of wine. Maybe it's a little over the top with all its mixed-berry pie filling and vanilla. But you know, there's comfort in all that excess sheet metal and buttery leather. And once you've uncorked the bottle and settled into the La-Z-Boy (or the lawn chair, considering this is big-time BBQ wine), life seems pretty comfortable after all.

 Maui ribs

 Chocolate cigars

Patio/Picnic, Classic

California

Maggio

2009 Petite Sirah
$18.99

I grew up in the southern California desert. Drive-ins, low-riders, and old soul tunes were everywhere. Especially each Sunday night, when Art Laboe's "Killer Oldies" show was dialled in and his selection of soulful tunes and heartfelt dedications caressed the airwaves. Now, Lodi may be in northern Cali, but you know it's got soul. And it has soulful wines like Maggio's Petite Sirah. A bright purple-garnet in the glass, it lingers with ripe black fruit and vanilla, soft and smooth through and through, with underlying toasty oak and smoke. It's a slow burner of a wine that urges leisurely lounging.

 On its own

 Machaca burritos

Rock out, BYO

Australia

Ringbolt

2010 Cabernet Sauvignon
$18.99

Cinnamon hearts and clove ciggies complement the rich black-currant fruit and menthol of this bold Cabernet Sauvignon. Ringbolt nicely captures the pure fruit and structured elegance common to the Margaret River region of Western Australia, traits owed to Margaret River's temperate, maritime climate. Pair with a fisherman sweater and grilled whole lamb leg to achieve maximum swagger.

 Grilled leg of lamb

 Quinoa and kale salad

Classic, Winter Warmer

Italy

Zonin

2010 Ripasso Valpolicella Superiore
$18.99

This bottle will forever represent an "aha" wine moment for me. It was the first Ripasso-style wine I tasted. On a restaurant patio in Seattle, in the prime of both my youth and summer! Ripasso (Italian for "repassed") is an ingenious form of recycling grapes. After high-end Amarone and Recioto are made, the leftover grape skins and pips (the pomace) are tossed into tanks of fermenting Valpolicella wine, giving the yeast additional grub that contributes to more colour, body, and character. So the resulting Ripasso is richer and bolder than typical Valpolicella, yet still fresh and approachable. Think bowlful of dried cherry and form-fitting velour.

 Mushroom risotto

 Roast pork

BYO, Romance

Spain

Terra de Falanis

2010 Muac!
$19.95

I have tasted exactly one wine from the island of Majorca (or in Spanish, Mallorca). But what I tasted makes me hope I come across more, and if you're looking for a red off the beaten path I suggest you give this a taste too. The Muac! is a lively blend of Callet, Manto Negro, and Cabernet Sauvignon grapes; the former two are native to this rocky outcropping in the Mediterranean and hence not part of the typical grape discussion. But this marvellous Mallorcan delights, from its cute comic-book label of a kissing couple (Muuuuuuaac!) to its rich dark fruit, earth, toasted spice, and fresh finish.

 Cabbage rolls

 Pan con tomate (aka bread with tomato)

Wine Geek, Patio/Picnic

Argentina

Amalaya

2010 Tinto
$19.99

A good blended wine is like a great soundtrack. Individual songs can capture a mood, but overall the whole album should work together to encapsulate a theme. Case in point, this "mainly Malbec" blend sports a listing of four grapes (75% Malbec, 15% Cabernet Sauvignon, and 5% each of Syrah and Tannat), and they come together in a harmonious medley of aromatic plum and violet bolstered by a plush mid-palate and a bold but firm, grippy finish. In short, the Amalaya sings in the glass.

 Pot-au-feu

 Aged Gouda

Patio/Picnic, Rock Out

France

Cave de Rasteau

2010 La Domelière Rasteau
$19.99

The red wines of Rasteau got promoted to AOC status (appellation d'origine contrôlée) from the 2009 vintage, making Rasteau one of France's newest protected regions of origin. While this is not quite like getting knighted and adding a "Sir" to your surname, it does raise Rasteau above the more generic Côtes du Rhône Villages riff-raff. It may even get the bottles into the VIP lineup at the club. You'll certainly feel dignified sipping this seriously tasty Rasteau. From a ripe, fruity entry it builds to a bold-yet-elegant overall style with a savoury, herby (but amazingly fresh) finish.

 Ratatouille

 Morbier

Wine Geek, Romance

Chile

Concha y Toro

2009 Marques de Casa Concha
Cabernet Sauvignon
$19.99

This is the wool blanket of wines. It will keep you warm through winter, not to mention smother the taste buds with all sorts of plush fruit and toasty goodness. We're talking serious opulence—picture the grapes growing in their Puente Alto vineyards in the Alto Maipo near Santiago in sun- and moonlit glory, basking and soaking it all in. The resultant juice is ripe with voluptuous plum, cassis, and fig. The fruit isn't tamed by 14 months in French oak; it's magnified by coffee bean, vanilla, and tobacco. One sip and your taste buds will be happy and warm (but be careful, one bottle and they'll be fuzzy!).

 Beef pot pie

 Aged Piave

Winter Warmer, Classic

Ontario

G. Marquis

2010 The Silver Line Pinot Noir
$19.99

Pinot envy? While I'm certainly happy to have such a bounty of B.C.–produced bottles for ready consumption, it does seem a shame that the selection of wines from Ontario available west of the Rockies can be counted on both hands. Especially when one manages to sneak in and proves as tasty as G. Marquis's Silver Line Pinot Noir. From Niagara-on-the-Lake (holla!).

This rich Pinot gushes with bright berry fruit and a smoky vanilla underlay. With a vibrant mid-palate and a punchy finish featuring nicely integrated toasty oak, it makes you wonder what other bottles we're missing out on.

 Lamb ragù over pasta

 Tomato ragù over pasta

Rock Out, Patio/Picnic

Argentina

La Posta

2010 Pizzella Family Vineyard Malbec
$19.99

File this Malbec under provenance! Argentina → Mendoza → Uco Valley → La Consulta → Finca Coquena → Pizzella Family Vineyard. La Posta clearly cares where the grapes for their Malbec come from, calling out the Pizzella Family Vineyard right on the front label. Actually, it's neat to break down where a wine comes from. It builds appreciation for the potential nuance and character possible in every bottle. In this particular case, the provenance means: raspberry and bramble aromatics up front → bright and lively mid-palate highlighting the vineyard's cooler-climate area → fresh, balanced finish. File this Malbec under *delicious!*

 Beef donburi

 Aged goat

Classic, BYO

Italy

Re Manfredi

2007 Aglianico del Vulture
$19.99

If you're looking for a red wine off the beaten path, consider this gutsy red from the Basilicata region deep in Italy's south. As the name conveniently describes, this wine is produced from Aglianico grapes grown in the volcanic soils of Vulture. This late-ripening grape is known for creating full-bodied, rich wines that can come across harsh when young. But with five years behind it, the Re Manfredi is boldly approachable with nuances of plum, earth, and spice. It's velvety but gruff along the edges—kind of like Scarlett Johansson's voice—and just as alluring. Stoke the charcoal and prep the mixed grill.

 Spicy Italian sausage

 Baba ghanoush

Patio/Picnic, Wine Geek

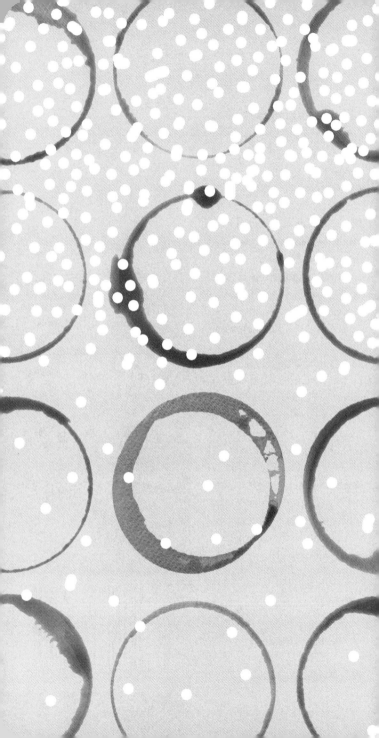

The Sparkling

Spain

Jaume Serra

N/V Cristalino Brut Cava
$12.99

"Sh'bam. Pow. Plop. Wizzz!" Whenever I pop the cork on a bottle of bubbly, Brigitte Bardot's little ditty from the classic Serge Gainsbourg track "Comic Strip" races through my head. Can't help it—it's a fun song, and sipping on sparkling always makes for a good time. Come to think of it, grabbing a couple dozen fresh oysters, gathering a shucking party, tossing Gainsbourg on the playlist, and cracking open a bottle of this Brut Cava would make for an excellent time indeed.

 Oysters on the half shell

 Seven-layer bean dip

Rock Out, BYO

Australia

Innocent Bystander

2010 Moscato
$13.99 for 375mL

Dessert wine doesn't need to be rich and heavy. This little number is just the opposite; it's light and striking to look at thanks to a gorgeous pink hue, artsy watercolour-bedecked label, and golden crown cap. It's also lightly spritzy! Gregarious aromas of honey, orange blossom, and raisins explode out of the glass, and with a tame 5.5 percent alcohol this sweet and fruity wine is certainly gulp-worthy. For an easy—yet amazingly romantic—dessert, pair it with pear, either freshly sliced or poached in vanilla syrup.

 On its own

 Poached pear

Romance, Wine Geek

Hungary

Hungaria

N/V Grande Cuvée Brut
$14.95

Whatever happened to crunk?
I miss the big sloppy beats, the effervescent call-and-response and over-the-top sparkle of bling. Getting your sip on with Hungaria is like having Lil Jon grinning in your grill. It's a crunk-worthy sparkler that's a little rough around the edges but boasts full-on flavour. With brioche notes, a nutty demeanour, and a bright lemon-meets-mineral finish, this budget sparkler oozes catchy character not typical at this price point. To which I toast: "Yea-ah!"

 Truffled popcorn

 Jalapeño Pepper Poppers

Rock Out, Patio/Picnic

Casolari

N/V Lambrusco di Sorbara
$14.99

If you haven't tried a sparkling red wine you're missing out. Sparkling Shiraz is the Christmas wine of choice in Australia, where plus-40 degree temperatures make cold turkey and a cold fizzy flute of red bubbly a festive and refreshing choice. Then there's frothy Lambrusco, the Italian sparkling red that's a primo *aperitivo*. For a great introduction to this fun style of wine, check out Casolari's taste-bud-tingling Lambrusco, which has rich cherry and floral notes crammed into the most vibrant shade of ruby possible. Show up with this bottle to your next dinner party and heads will turn.

 On its own

 Flatbread

Classic, BYO

Langa

N/V Real de Aragón Brut Cava
$14.99

Bubbly is a time-honoured brunch-wine choice. Not only does it mix well with OJ and most other fruit juices for leisurely morning sipping, but thanks to its higher acidity and palate-scrubbing bubbles, sparkling wine tends to match up nicely with egg dishes. A recent arrival from Spain, the non-vintage Real de Aragón Cava is quite rich and fizzes with a frothy mousse. Aromas of apple, lemon, and nuts lead to nice toasted notes and a tart finish. It's a great value that looks classy to boot.

 On its own (or mixed with OJ)

 Egg white frittata

BYO, Patio/Picnic

Argentina

1884 Reservado

N/V Extra Brut
$17.99

Top ten ways to enjoy this easygoing, extroverted Argentine sparkler: 10) with a fluted glass; 9) with eggs Benedict at Sunday brunch; 8) with equal parts OJ; 7) with crab cakes to start a meal; 6) to toast a promotion; 5) to turn a frown upside down; 4) with meatloaf on Wednesday; 3) with a splash of crème de cassis for a kir royale; 2) with strawberries as an impromptu dessert; 1) with a good friend and an evening to converse.

 On its own

 Unagi

Wednesday Wine, BYO

Italy

Beato Bartolomeo Breganze

N/V Rosa di Sera Spumante
Extra Dry
$19.99

Don't forget the sparkling rosé!
The Rosa di Sera pours a
radiant, captivating cherry
blossom blush in the glass that
screams party in pink as it
bubbles over with berry and
citrus aromas. There's an evident
sweetness in this wine, but it's
balanced by a crisp finish and
the natural refreshment of fizz.
If you're looking to find a fun
sparkler that goes down easy,
either sipped solo or alongside
BBQ ribs, you've found it.

 Maui ribs

 Turkish delight

Patio/Picnic, Romance

Italy

Tranchero

2011 Moscato d'Asti
$19.99

Rappers may have Champagne, but emo kids have Moscato d'Asti. Or at least they should drink it. Sweet yet sincere, Moscato d'Asti evokes instant emotion, calling out to be embraced and enjoyed on first sip. It tickles the tongue with light effervescence but lacks the in-your-face fizz of sparkling wine. Plus, a bottle of Moscato d'Asti won't break the bank, and let's face it, there's nothing more earnest than wining on a budget. Tranchero's Moscato d'Asti gives you a full-sized bottle for under a 20, and it's full of peach, 7-Up, and orange blossom but has enough acidity on the finish to keep things fresh (and true).

 On its own

 Ricotta-filled cannoli

Rock Out, Romance

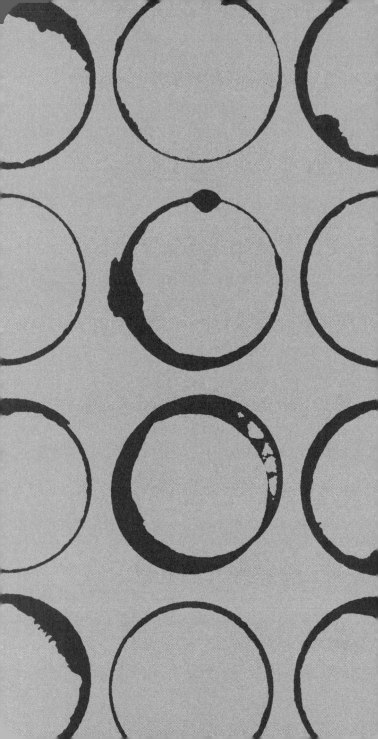

The Fortifieds

Italy

Cinzano

N/V Rosso
$12.75 for 1 L

An aperitif is truly a civilized way to start a meal. Really, there's no better way to get the gastronomical juices going. Vermouth, the fortified wine spiked with bitter herbs and aromatics, makes a classic aperitif, either on its own or as an integral ingredient in a pre-dinner cocktail. Sating since the mid-18th century, Cinzano Rosso is a classic in its own right. A beguiling bitterness is set off by a rich sweetness in this easy-to-get-into sipping vermouth with fantastic herbal, coriander, and camomile tones complemented by citrus. Keep a bottle in the fridge door, and an hour or two before dinner splash a couple ounces into a wineglass, then top with a lemon twist.

 On its own

 Bowl of peanuts

Patio/Picnic, BYO

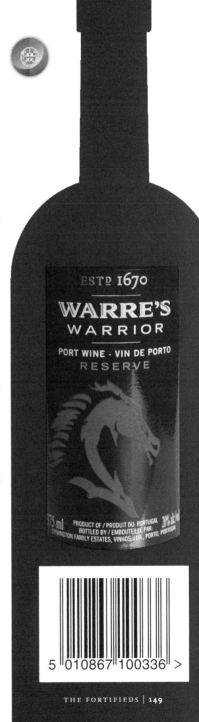

Warre's

N/V Warrior Reserve Port
$12.99 for 375 mL

Warrior Reserve is a pretty badass name for a wine, but then this is not ordinary wine. It's fortified wine from the renowned terraced slopes of the Douro Valley. Huzzah! It dares the other wines to come out and play. In fact, according to Warre's, their Warrior is the oldest port brand in the world. The name has been emblazoned onto the firm's casks since the port house's earliest days back in the 17th century. But don't worry, out of the bottle and in the glass the Warrior Reserve is actually an easygoing, everyday port bursting with lush dark fruit and a plush richness that calls for a companion, good conversation, and a night without interruption.

 Stilton

 Dark chocolate brownies

Romance, Classic

Spain

Alvear

N/V Fino
$14.99

I don't know what it was like to participate in three-martini lunches (I honestly don't think I'd get any work done the rest of the day). And I'm no Don Draper with a stocked bar cart of Canadian Club in my office. But I do feel that a four-o'clock "Fino Stop" is a beautiful thing, a great way to gather the troops and go over the day's successes and failures, opportunities and challenges, and perhaps strategize for the pending morrow. An ounce or two of this nutty, lip-smacking, and bone-dry fortified will do—preferably served with almonds and/or a nibble of cheese. It's a little ritual that adds class and comfort to the workplace.

 Pan-toasted almonds

 Manchego

Classic, Wednesday Wine

Spain

González Byass

N/V Nutty Solera Oloroso Sherry
$16.99

Nutty Solera is like the awl on a Swiss Army knife. Not many people ever use it, but it's actually a pretty useful little tool to have in the kit. You can use it to punch a new hole in a belt or stitch up a pair of moccasins. In desperate times it even serves as a cork- screw of last resort. Nutty Solera is an Oloroso, or "scented," sherry, imbued with the great amber colour and nutty nuances from its unique oxidative winemaking process. It's a darn fine after- dinner tipple, particularly with nuts and/or a cheese plate, ideally served in the lounge post-pran- dial. Best of all, it comes topped with a reusable cork plug—no corkscrew required!

 Gruyère

 Peanut brittle

Winter Warmer, Romance

Lillet

N/V
$16.99

I'd like to amend my rule concerning a basic wine collection. To the previously suggested bottle each of white, red, and sparkling I add a bottle of Lillet. Keep it in the fridge along with the white and sparkling to be ready for any of life's occasions (and to ensure you follow the label's clear instructions to "Serve Well Chilled"). Then, when the moment for an aperitif calls, pour a couple ounces of Lillet over a few rocks, twist a lemon peel, and kick off the shoes. Or, if it's time for a cocktail, consider the Corpse Reviver No. 2: 1 oz gin, 1 oz Cointreau, 1 oz Lillet, 1 oz fresh lemon juice, and a scant dash absinthe.

On its own

Wednesday Wine, Classic

Notes

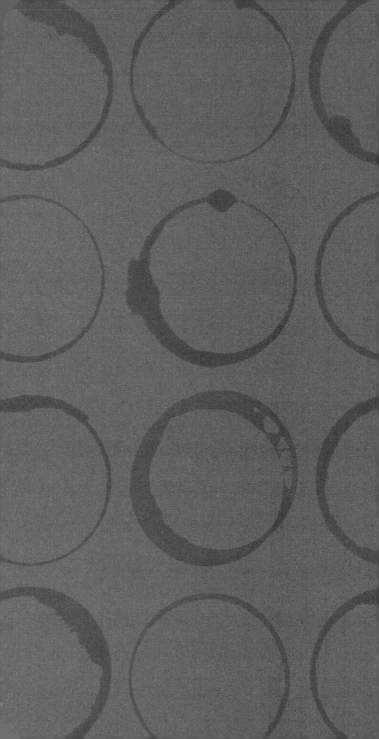

The Splurge

Had a Glass famously champions the idea that there is a wine for every occasion and every budget. Well, occasionally it's necessary to blow the budget! The plain truth is that certain types of wine will never fall into the under-$20 category. This doesn't mean they're not good value. It just means most of us won't be buying these bottles on a daily basis! But for those times that warrant crossing the threshold, here is a brief look at some wines worthy of a splurge. They may be harder to find, but they're worth the hunt.

Splurge #1: Plus-sized bottles

For wine, size matters. The standard-sized, 750 mL bottle is just fine for everyday use. However, some occasions may call for a magnum (1.5 L), or even something larger. While it's true that you will be a star if you show up at a dinner party with a plus-sized bottle, there is also strategy behind going big. Larger bottles age differently than regular bottles—they are said to age more slowly thanks to a smaller oxygen-to-liquid ratio with the air trapped inside the bottle (the ullage). When you're ready to tackle a larger cork, try heaving one of these three options:

Jean Foillard Cote du Py Morgon, France (~$89 for 1.5L)
Osoyoos Larose Le Grand Vin, British Columbia (~$100 for 1.5L)
Caymus Special Selection Cabernet Sauvignon, California
    (~$269 for 1.5L)

Splurge #2: Champagne

We're talking capital C Champagne, the sparkling wine made in the Champagne region of France. It's the bubbly without peer that unfortunately carries peerless prices. A half-bottle costs at least $35, and the cheapest bottle runs around $50. However, for life's moments that clamour for the epitome of classic celebration, you might just consider cracking open the Champers.

Non-vintage bottles from large Champagne producers, like Moët & Chandon Imperial (~$65) and Bollinger Special Cuvée (~$75), offer wine made from a blend of various years in order to maintain a consistent flavour profile. These are the most common Champagne picks.

For more pomp with your pop, opt for vintage Champagne. You'll know its vintage when a specific year is labelled, which means that all the grapes used to make the Champagne come from the same harvest. Vintage Champagne typically equals more character and more prestige, and henceforth a higher price tag. Try Louis Roederer 2004 Cristal Brut (~$275) when you're feeling plucky.

Along with the noble Champagne houses, also keep in mind the Grower Champagne labels. Many of these smaller, independent Champagne producers have gained loyal followings, such as Champagne Paul Bara Brut Rosé (~$60).

Splurge #3: Vintage port

There are many types of port, and each has its place. See the review of Warre's Warrior (on page 149) for a great Reserve Port that is ready for everyday drinking. There's also Tawny Port, which spends significant time in oak barrels and takes on tawny hues and caramel notes from its sojourn in wood. But then there's Vintage Port, the port you put away for decades that can easily outlive a lifetime. Vintage Port needs time in the bottle to fully develop its delicious potential. It's a special wine, but it's not cheap—expect to pay at minimum $60 for a regular-sized bottle.

Niepoort Vintage 2007, Portugal (~$50 for 375mL)
Graham Vintage 2000, Portugal (~$80 for 375mL)
Fonseca Vintage 2007, Portugal (~$125)

Splurge #4: Or for that matter, a bottle of any good ol' sticky, fortified wine

While you will find a few fortified wine picks under $20, it's fair to say the pickings are slim in this price range. Really, for a few dollars more your world of fortified wine gets wide open: Marsala, Madeira, sherry, *vin doux naturel*, not to mention fortified wines from outside the Old World. The options are myriad, and fortifieds are a class of wine really worth appreciating. Plus, they're consumed in small servings so the bottle tends to go further.

Lustau East India Solera Sherry, Spain (~$21 for 375mL)
Marnier Lapostolle Pineau des Charentes, France (~$22)
Blandy's Duke of Clarence Madeira, Portugal (~$27)

Splurge #5: Go au naturel!

Natural, naked, authentic (insert stripped-down adjective here) wine has really gained attention—and infamy. Proponents like the dedication to organic and biodynamic farming, and the strict adherence to minimal intervention and lack of chemicals and additives during winemaking. Critics contend there is nothing natural about wine in the first place; if left alone, grape juice would rot into vinegar. Regardless, the unfortunate truth is that you're not likely to find *vin naturel* on shelves in Canada for under $20 (though you will find a number of wines made from organically grown grapes). Curious?

Marcel Lapierre Morgon, France (~$35) is a Cru Beaujolais with authentic character.

Avis de Vin Fort, France (~$27) is made by the Loire Valley's Catherine and Pierre Breton.

Broadside Cabernet Sauvignon, California (~$30) hails from the Paso Robles region and is made without commercial yeasts or the addition of any bacteria or acid.

Splurge #6: Top-tier Riesling

With renewed interest in craftsmanship and provenance, is Riesling's time to shine right around the corner? A longtime favourite of sommeliers and wine professionals, Riesling still hasn't widely caught on. But there's no wine better at showcasing purity and a sense of place, and while you'll find a handful of Rieslings in the top 100, spend a few dollars beyond $20 and you'll be treated to top-notch expressions of the grape from world-renowned vineyards in Germany, France, and Australia. (Bonus: Quality Riesling ages beautifully.)

Pewsey Vale Eden Valley Riesling, Australia (~$24)

Schlumberger Les Princes Abbes Riesling, France (~$26)

Joh. Jos. Prüm Wehlener Sonnenuhr Riesling Spätlese, Germany (~$58)

Splurge #7: Gran Reserva Rioja

Speaking of aging wine, the classic red wines of Spain are aged for you at the winery. Legally, any Spanish wine labelled *Reserva* must age for a minimum of three years before release (at least one of which is in oak barrels); *Gran Reserva* must rest for a staggering five years before hitting shelves (24 months in barrel and a further

36 months in bottle). Of course, thanks to this leisurely soak in oak and the inventory holding costs at the winery, this laboured liquid of love comes at a price. You'll find one Gran Reserva from the region of Valdepeñas earlier in this book (on page 96), while the Reservas and Gran Reservas recommended here are from Rioja—Spain's most acclaimed wine locale. All showcase great value and cut out the need for a "best after" date!

Marques de Riscal Rioja Reserva, Spain (~$29)
Muga Rioja Reserva, Spain (~$29)
Remelluri Gran Reserva Rioja, Spain (~$75)

Splurge #8: Grand Cru Burgundy

There may very well come a time in your wine career when you fall madly for Pinot Noir. This is OK—it's to be expected. Pinot Noir is unscientifically proven to be the wine grape most people go gaga over. It is also, sadly, not the most affordable wine around. When you find yourself Pinot smitten, odds are you'll eventually want to head to the heartland. Burgundy is one of the world's most complicated regions, known to test both intellect and pocketbook. But Burgundy *does* produce some ethereal Pinot Noir, and Grand Cru Burgundy is considered the best of the best. So gather some friends, pool your resources, splurge on Burgundy, and make it an event to remember.

Domaine d'Eugenie Échezeaux, France (~$300)
Clos de Tart, France (~$500)
Domaine de la Romanée-Conti, France (a.k.a. DRC) (around, ahem, $10,000—if you can find a bottle!)

Splurge #9: A bottle from your birth year

Enjoying a bottle from your birth year makes for a truly unforgettable wine experience. However, unless your parents were wise enough to think ahead and squirrel away a case or two to celebrate the birth of their child, odds are you'll rarely come across appropriately-aged bottles. So when you do pass that wine shop with the vintage in question, or perhaps see it listed online, think hard before passing it up—but do make sure it has been properly cellared. Here are a couple of ideas to keep in mind:

Bordeaux and other Cabernet blends can go the distance and age gracefully (just like you, right?).

Grand Cru Chablis ages well and is the perfect choice if white wine is more your style (from $50 and up).

Or try an aforementioned Riesling.

Splurge #10: A coffee-table-worthy wine reference book

Had a Glass is the guide for everyday wine enjoyment. And if you find yourself enjoying wine more and more each day, it's worth investing in a great wine reference book that gets further into the nitty-gritty of this fine beverage. Sure, you could probably go online and get all the required information. But a book is classy, easy to use, and allows you to stumble onto unexpected things with the simple flip of the page (plus, you don't have to worry about spilling wine on the keyboard).

The Oxford Companion to Wine (Oxford University Press, 3rd edition, 2006) was compiled and edited by renowned Master of Wine, Jancis Robinson. It is a time-tested compendium covering the gamut—from viticulture to types of wine and every piece of wine esoterica in between—all in an easy-to-use, A-to-Z encyclopedic format.

The World Atlas of Wine (Mitchell Beazley, 6th edition, 2007) by Hugh Johnson and Jancis Robinson presents amazingly detailed maps of all the major wine regions, alongside interesting, colourful write-ups detailing the history and importance of each locale.

Notes

Index by Country

Index by Type

Acknowledgements

Had a Glass would experience stuck fermentation if not for a large contingent of supportive, creative, and talented people.

First and foremost, I'd like to raise my glass to all the readers. Your support and inquisitive thirst keep me swirling and sipping!

Thanks to Robert, Lindsay, and the entire Appetite team for giving me the opportunity and providing the platform to bring Had a Glass to life, and a fist bump to Grace for making me mind my Ps and Qs.

Cin cin to the wineries, agents, and wine shops striving to bring new and exciting wines to our market while remaining committed to new vintages of classic value bottles. My dentist deserves a shout-out for keeping my enamel in check—no easy feat considering the quantity of wine tasting. And a yeoman's holler to Le Marché St. George, the best little neighbourhood grocer that is nothing short of an oasis in East Van.

Respect is due to Kenji, my partner in wine crime. You are missed in geography but never feel far away. Had a Glass will always remain as much a legacy of your creative energies. May your Grolleau, Cab Franc, and Chenin vines continue to grow strong and free.

I also want to acknowledge the venues that have long given me space and column inches to spread the wine love, in particular the Province newspaper and Taste magazine.

Finally, thank you to my family and friends. The former has cellar-worthy patience, the latter cellar-worthy thirst, and together you provide an amazing support network that makes this book possible.

JAMES NEVISON is an award-winning wine writer, educator, and the co-founder of HALFAGLASS wine consultancy in Vancouver. James has co-authored five best-selling wine books, and he is widely known as "The Wine Guy" from his weekly column in The Province newspaper. James also contributes regularly to Taste magazine, and his casual and accessible take on wine is often heard and seen on radio and television. James has judged wine competitions in Canada and internationally, and he was honoured to be named one of Western Living magazine's "Top 40 Foodies Under 40."